MATTERS OF LIFE AND DEATH

MATTERS OF
LIFE AND DEATH

An Inquiry into
Spiritualism, Faith Healing and Psychic Research Today

BY

GEOFFREY MURRAY

With an Introduction by
THE DEAN OF ST. PAUL'S

SIDGWICK AND JACKSON LIMITED
LONDON

First published 1953

MADE AND PRINTED IN GREAT BRITAIN BY PURNELL AND SONS, LTD.
PAULTON (SOMERSET) AND LONDON

CONTENTS

INTRODUCTION

I HAVE read Mr. Murray's book with great interest. He has attempted a difficult task in surveying a wide area of alleged new knowledge and experience and giving an account which will be intelligible to those who have no acquaintance with the writings of specialists. Anyone who is concerned to keep in touch with the development of thought must take note of the progress of psychical research and the related subjects of faith-healing and spiritualism. In my opinion, we are on the verge of important new insight into the nature of human personality as a result of recent discoveries in the field of para-normal psychology. There is a danger that conclusions may be too hastily drawn from the accumulating evidence, and I am in cordial agreement with Mr. Murray when he suspends judgment on many of the more extreme claims made for the spiritualist hypothesis, but it seems clear that telepathy, clairvoyance, and extra-sensory perception are well-established phenomena and, though the mode of their operation is obscure, they throw light upon the personality of man. One conclusion at least appears to emerge. Any materialistic conception of the self and its powers becomes increasingly difficult to maintain. In this respect, at least, the new knowledge is in harmony with religious faith. I would go further and suggest that the phenomena of clairvoyance and E.S.P. tend to show that the common-sense idea of the situation of the self in space and time will need drastic revision.

Both philosophy and theology must, in the long run, be affected by the new data about the human mind and its scope, for both must grapple with the question, *What is man?* Philosophers, such as Professors C. D. Broad and H. H. Price, have begun to consider the bearing of the results of psychical research on the nature of mind and its place in reality, but I find no comparable effort on the part of theologians. I regret that the Report of the Commission appointed by the

Archbishops to investigate the relation of Spiritualism to the Christian faith was not published, because a considerable amount of careful thought was expended on it, but perhaps the most fruitful way of dealing with the problem would be that individual theologians, who commit no one but themselves, should try to explore the possibilities. I have attempted something of the kind in my recent book, the *Problem of Christ in the Twentieth Century,* in which I have ventured to employ some results of psychical research in a restatement of the doctrine of the Incarnation. But it is evident that no doctrine of the Christian Faith can be aloof from the consequences of changed views of the nature of human personality, and the new knowledge needs to be incorporated into our interpretation of the Atonement and Redemption. This will certainly be a long and arduous undertaking—but it should be taken in hand now.

Dr. Rhine is right when he says that we know more about the atom than about ourselves, and it may well be that the next great advance in knowledge will be in the sphere of psychology and the philosophy of mind. No doubt we shall learn much more about our mysterious selves and we may hope that the knowledge will be used for good and not for evil. Just as knowledge about the atom can be used either creatively or destructively, so can knowledge of the powers of the mind. It would be an error to suppose that exploration of the recesses of the personality will give us either the will or the power to become saints and sages. Nor do I think that we shall ever clear up the mystery of the self. It is misleading to compare the mind with the atom, for the situation is really quite different. The atom is a supposed object which we attempt to know. The self is both subject and object. Man trying to know himself is playing two parts at the same time—the knower and the known. For this reason I believe that, however much our knowledge is extended, the human ego will always remain the ultimate mystery, that which most certainly exists and is the subject of all knowledge and experience, but itself can be intuited yet never known.

The Deanery, St. Paul's.   W. R. MATTHEWS.

FOREWORD

CURIOUSLY, because of the popular interest taken in it, there is no word in common English usage that precisely delineates the subject treated in this book. The specialist, it is true, has been forced to invent terms so as to grapple with the phenomena here described, but these terms have not yet found their way into the language of ordinary men and women. Extra-sensory perception (abbreviated to E.S.P.), *psi* phenomena, precognition, psychokinesis or PK, and even the American portmanteau word, para-psychology, are all jargon in most people's ears and forbidding when not utterly meaningless. It is, therefore, a matter of considerable difficulty to indicate in a word the scope of this book. Spiritualism is too narrow in its connotation for my purpose, and so is psychical research, though the fault here lies largely with most laymen who have debased the term to imply solely the investigation of the genuineness of mediums and the nature of poltergeistic manifestations: in truth, psychic research has many more sides to it than those. Contrariwise, occultism and abnormal psychology are both too wide and loose in their significance to define with the necessary precision the nature of this particular book. Somewhere between these extremes lies the subject of the present inquiry. Spiritualism certainly comes into a great deal of it. So, too, does orthodox Christianity. And so does the abnormal psychology which treats of hypnosis, suggestion, and trance conditions. Psychic research, a no-man's-land of science, has naturally to be considered. There is some theology, a glance at materialism, and even an account of the law and law-making. Yet there is no one word to indicate how this apparently strange mixture is fused into a unity of its own.

With the legalisation in 1951 of Spiritualism in Britain, an opportunity seemed to be presented for elucidating the development and present standing of—what shall I say, psychic research, para-psychology, or belief in survival and a future life? The topicality of such an inquiry was increased by the approaching centenary of the first seances to be held in this country: it seemed well worth-while to find out what has been achieved in a hundred years of sitting with mediums and of the criticisms of this practice. And since the most active seekers after psychic phenomena—though not always the most scientific in spirit and training—are Spiritualists, a beginning was made by studying how Spiritualism and psychic research (for there is a deep cleavage between the two) have grown and matured, how they are organised and practised, and how their teachings or conclusions have merged and crystallised.

It soon became plain, however, that the inquiry could not end there, for both Spiritualism and psychic research have impinged sharply upon orthodox Christianity, philosophy, and science, and it was inevitable that the effect of this should be studied. Anglican, Roman Catholic, and Nonconformist churchmen all nowadays treat with respect the Spiritualist doctrine of survival after death, though some of them reject, often with contumely, the theology of Spiritualism. Similarly, the investigation by professional psychologists of telepathy, hypnosis, and telekinesis have provided rationalistic authority for a good deal of clairvoyance and mediumship. Accordingly, all this had to be brought within the purview of my study. Then, since it was my ambition to make a strictly impartial survey, attention had finally to be directed to the reasoned scepticism of those who reject the hypothesis that mediumship enables communication to take place with the spirits of the dead. In the last chapter I have taken the risk of describing, though with many hesitancies, my own point of view as it formed in the course of my inquiry—a risk, I say, because it must expose me to the fire of believers and non-believers alike.

This book has evolved out of a series of articles I wrote in the *News Chronicle* soon after the General Election of 1951.

We on the staff of that newspaper had been impressed by the way in which the political battle had resolved itself into a conflict over material issues—food subsidies, vegetable marketing, and the amount of "red meat" which the contending parties were willing to promise the electors. The clash of principles which had marked politics in the past seemed to have vanished, and for relief from the drab materiality which characterised the election campaign of 1951 we turned to contemplate some things of the spirit. Thus the series of articles was born. To Mr. R. J. Cruikshank, Editor of the *News Chronicle,* the "onlie begetter" of the articles, I extend my warmest thanks for his inspiration and encouragement, and for permitting me to use in this book material that originally appeared in the newspaper he edits.

To another colleague, Mr. Hugh Redwood, Religious Editor of the *News Chronicle,* I owe the suggestion that I should widen the inquiry and embrace the work of the Church in the fields of divine, faith, and Christian healing in contrast to psychic or Spiritualistic healing. Redwood opened many doors for me and increased my indebtedness to him by reading, and advising on, part of the MS.

I cannot easily acknowledge how great is my debt of gratitude to Mr. Ralph Rossiter, secretary of the Marylebone Spiritualist Association, for all the help he gave me and for the immense trouble he cheerfully went to on my behalf. Mr. Rossiter arranged for me to sit with seven different mediums. He guided me through the vast literature Spiritualism has evoked, and he answered with unruffled patience, and with no little humour, my many questions.

Mr. Harry Edwards, the psychic healer, allowed me to watch him, in the closest possible proximity, at work throughout an entire afternoon, and so did another Spiritualist healer, Mrs. Nan Mackenzie. Lord Dowding submitted to my interrogation during a meeting of the Obsession Circle of the M.S.A. Mr. Richard Ellidge, secretary of the Spiritualists' National Union, Mr. H. F. Bendall, president of the Greater World Christian Spiritualist League, and Mr. Ivan Cooke, of the White Eagle Lodges, all generously supplied me with pamphlets and other statements relating to their organisations. Professor J. B. Rhine, of Duke University, North Carolina, in response to a cable, at once sent to me by air mail a mass of documents relating to his latest work and that of his colleagues. This was a particularly rich vein that I was glad to work. Professor Rhine's was a most generous gesture.

The Rev. W. E. Sangster, of Central Hall, Westminster, gave up a morning to answering my questions, and so did the Rev. C. Barker, of Hove. Hannah Leather, of Horsham, Sussex, gave me invaluable information relating to the Society of Friends' concern for spiritual healing.

Finally, Dr. C. E. M. Joad bestowed on me the benefit of his stimulating and questing mind at one unforgettable luncheon. His discourse was so engrossing that we were both wildly late for our respective appointments.

I thank each of these people for their help, advice, and co-operation, at the same time completely exonerating them from all responsibility for any errors of fact or distortion of opinion that may have crept into this book. In numerous instances I have wilfully disregarded their more expert and informed conclusions in favour of my own, and possibly rash, opinion, believing it to be more honest in this account of one plain seeker's findings to advance my own views rather than accept theirs at second hand.

CHAPTER I

WITCHCRAFT INTO MEDIUMSHIP

O N June 22, 1951, the Fraudulent Mediums Act became law and a long-standing stigma was removed from the people called Spiritualists by taking them out of the legal categories of witches and vagrants. The Act, so drafted that it has none of the jargon that usually makes the will of Parliament incomprehensible to laymen, is commendably short, for it is contained on a single octavo sheet, of which a copy can be bought from His Majesty's Stationery Office for twopence. But it marks, as most of those stressed who took part in the House of Commons debate that preceded its passing, the completion of the movement for religious toleration that began, in 1669, with the Toleration Act and was progressively extended by the Catholic Emancipation Act of 1829, the admission of Jews to Parliament in 1858, and the abolition of Church rates in 1868. From that slow movement towards religious freedom Spiritualists were excluded primarily because of the late origin of their beliefs. Mediumship was not practised in this country until 1853, and although Robert Browning inveighed against "Mr. Sludge, 'The Medium'" and the young H. G. Wells was another trenchant critic, it was not until the 1914 war that Spiritualists ceased to be more than a small, disregarded sect occasionally patronised by High Society when in search of an intellectual thrill. True, that sect had included men of the calibre of Darwin's fellow-worker, Alfred Russel Wallace, of Sir William Crookes, the venerable Robert Owen of New Lanark, Professors Henry Sidgwick of Cambridge, and Lord Balfour, the brother of A. J. Balfour, the Prime Minister. Later adherents were to include Sir Oliver Lodge and Sir Arthur Conan Doyle, but for the first fifty years of its existence the Spiritualist movement was weak and puny.

13

The prey of many charlatans, it had to struggle desperately to survive, and was nursed through its sickly infancy by such passionate believers as F. W. H. Myers, Edward Gurney, and the Rev. W. Stainton Moses. These upholders were, by comparison with the present numerical strength of the Spiritualists, pitifully few. Modern states are not inclined to protect tiny, struggling minorities whom the rest of the nation dismiss as cranks, fools, or even perverts. So it was with Spiritualists. If an ancient Act could be invoked by their opponents to brand them, well so be it. There were few champions to intervene on behalf of the derided believers.

Paradoxically, however, the Witchcraft Act of 1735, which left Spiritualists naked to the sword of the Law, had been designed as a measure of enlightenment embodying the spirit of the Age of Reason. It was passed to testify to the eighteenth century's sturdy rationalism that witchcraft was hocus-pocus and that if any boasted they practised it then they were, *ipso facto*, frauds. From time immemorial mankind has been prone to believe in the existence of discarnate spirits. Sir James Frazer's *The Golden Bough* is crowded with instances. Both the Old and the New Testaments dilate on the subject. We read, for instance, of the Witch of Endor whom Saul consulted after he "had put away those that had familiar spirits, and the wizards, out of the land". Yet one remained, the woman of Endor, and before he went to her in his distress Saul disguised himself and put on other raiment, so that she would not recognise him as the King.

" 'I pray thee,' " Saul told her when they met, " 'divine unto me by the familiar spirit, and bring me him up, whom I shall name unto thee.'

"And the woman said unto him, 'Behold, thou knowest what Saul hath done, how he hath cut off those that have familiar spirits, and the wizards, out of the land: wherefore then layest thou a snare for my life, to cause me to die?'

"And Saul swore to her by the Lord, saying, 'As the Lord liveth, there shall no punishment happen to thee for this thing.'

"Then said the woman, 'Whom shall I bring up unto thee?'

"And he said, 'Bring me up Samuel.'

"And when the woman saw Samuel, she cried with a loud voice. And the woman spoke to Saul, saying, 'Why hast thou deceived me? for thou art Saul.'

"And the King said unto her, 'Be not afraid; for what sawest thou?' And the woman said unto Saul, 'I saw gods ascending out of the earth.'

"And he said unto her, 'What form is he of?' And she said, 'An old man cometh up; and he is covered with a mantle.' And Saul perceived it was Samuel, and he stooped with his face to the ground, and bowed himself.

"And Samuel said to Saul, 'Why hast thou disquieted me, to bring me up?'

"And Saul answered, 'I am sore distressed, for the Philis·tines make war against me, and God is departed from me and answereth me no more, neither by prophets nor by dreams. Therefore I have called thee, that thou mayest make known unto me what I shall do.'"

The outcome of that seance so terrified Saul that he was prostrated. The Biblical writers are, on the whole, merciless towards witches. There is the forthright commandment: "Thou shalt not suffer a witch to live." And the Prophets, over and over again, attribute the afflictions of the Children of Israel to God's displeasure at their traffickings with soothsayers, witches, and wizards—all people who were believed to have made partnerships with the Devil or the powers of darkness, their "familiar spirits", in return for supernatural capacities.

St. Paul, however, is believed by some people to have taken a more lenient view of those who, in the modern term, are "psychic". They base this opinion on the passage in his Epistle to the Corinthians in which St. Paul wrote: "Now concerning spiritual gifts, brethren, I would not have you ignorant. . . . The manifestation of the Spirit is given to every man to profit withal. For to one is given by the Spirit the word of wisdom; to another the word of knowledge by the same Spirit; to another faith by the same Spirit; to another the gifts of healing by the same Spirit; to another the working of miracles; to another prophecy; to another discerning of spirits."

In England witch-hunts do not seem to have been at all commonplace until the sixteenth century, and even then there were some who did not share the contemporary attitude to witches. Shakespeare certainly attributed prophetic powers akin to those of the Delphic Oracle to his witches in *Macbeth*, but there is nothing in the text, nor in Macbeth's own behaviour, to suggest that Shakespeare believed in the reality of his weird sisters. They were a dramatic convention like the Pities in Hardy's *The Dynasts*.

But within Shakespeare's own lifetime feeling against witches mounted. It was popularly and firmly believed that these crones, in league with the Devil, were able, by means of spells, to engineer the deaths of those who crossed them. A race of witch-hunters, of whom the most notorious was Matthew Hopkins, sprang up in various parts of the country and they kept the hangmen busy by methods every whit as dubious as the enchantments that their victims were alleged to practise. While the scare lasted, hundreds of poor, half-crazed, ignorant old women ended their wretched lives on the gallows. Wizards fared better. The general attitude to magicians and witches was best expressed by King James I and VI in his *Daemonology*: "Magicians command the devils: witches are their servants." A striking instance of this differentiation is Prospero in *The Tempest,* the master of Ariel and Caliban.

The extermination of witches reached its peak during the Long Parliament and then rapidly abated. From the Restoration onwards a new spirit, one of dispassionate, scientific inquiry, was in control. Sir Isaac Newton, John Locke, Robert Boyle, Edmund Halley, John Evelyn, and the men who founded the Royal Society changed the intellectual standards of their time and taught their contemporaries to apply new critical techniques to what they saw, heard, or read. An example of this change is the account written by Sir John Reresby of a witch trial he attended in 1687 at York Assizes:

"A poor old woman had the hard fate to be condemned

for a witch. Some, that were more apt to believe those things than me, thought the evidence strong against her, the boy that said he was bewitched falling into fits before the bench when he see her. But in all this it was observed that the boy had no distortion, no foaming at the mouth, nor did his fits leave him gradually, but all of a sudden; so that the judge thought fit to reprieve her.

"However, it is just to relate this odd story. One of my soldiers, being upon the guard at eleven o'clock that night at Clifford Tower Gate the night the witch was arraigned, hearing a great noise at the castle, came to the porch, and being there see a scroll of paper creep from under the door, which as he imagined by moonshine, turned first into the shape of a monkey, then a turkey cock, which moved to and fro by him. Whereupon he went to the gaol and called the under-gaoler, who came and see the scroll dance up and down and creep under the door, where there was scarce the room of the thickness of half a crown. This I had from the mouth both of the soldier and gaoler."

The last execution for witchcraft took place in England in 1704. In Scotland it was in 1722. Thirteen years later Parliament agreed that it was time to repeal the Act passed in the first year of James I's reign "Against Conjuration, Witchcraft, and dealing with evil and wicked spirits", and instead, for it is rare for one Act to be repealed without the passing of another, to lay down punishments for "such Persons as pretend to exercise or use any Kind of Witchcraft, Sorcery, Inchantment, or Conjuration". For the next two hundred and fifteen years it was not witchcraft that was an offence against the law, but the *pretence* of "Witchcraft, Sorcery, Inchantment, or Conjuration". Evil spirits had been "abolished" by Act of Parliament. When, therefore, in a later day, a spiritualistic medium was charged under the Witchcraft Act he was legally debarred from demonstrating the powers he alleged he possessed before the court, because the law held that discarnate spirts were non-existent and could not be conjured up.

Moreover, the Witchcraft Act was not the only one of which Spiritualists fell foul. The Vagrancy Act of 1824 could also be invoked against them. It stemmed from Tudor and Elizabethan statutes aimed at suppressing "all idle persons feigning themselves to have knowledge of physiognomy, palmistry, or other like crafty science or order pretending that they can tell fortunes, destinies, or such other like fantastical imaginations". Such people, declared the Elizabethan statute, "shall be adjudged and deemed rogues, vagabonds, and sturdy beggars". Consequently it is not surprising that the 1824 Act should have read:

"And for the more effectual preventing and punishing any Pretences to such Arts or Powers as are before-mentioned, whereby ignorant Persons are frequently deluded and defrauded; Be it further enacted . . . That if any Person shall, from and after the said 24th day of June, pretend to exercise or use any Kind of Witchcraft, Sorcery, Inchantment, or Conjuration, or undertake to tell Fortunes, or pretend from his or her Skill or Knowledge in any occult or crafty Science to discover where or in what Manner any Goods or Chattels supposed to have been stolen or lost, may be found; every Person so offending . . . after having been convicted as an idle and disorderly Person; every Person pretending or professing to tell Fortunes, or using any subtle Craft, Means, or Device, by Palmistry or otherwise, to deceive or impose on His Majesty's subjects; every Person wandering abroad and lodging in any Barn or Outhouse, or in any deserted or unoccupied Building, or in the open Air or under a Tent, or in any Cart or Waggon, not having any visible Means of Subsistence, and not giving a Good Account of himself; every Person wilfully exposing to view, in any Street, Road, Highway, or public Place, any obscene Print, Picture, or indecent Exhibition; every Person wilfully, openly, lewdly and obscenely exposing his Person in any Street, Road, or public Highway, or in the view thereof, or in any Place of public Resort, with Intent to insult any Female; every Person wandering abroad and endeavouring by the exposure of Wounds or Deformities to obtain or gather Alms; every Person going about as a Gatherer or Collector of Alms, or endeavouring to procure Charitable Contributions of any Nature or Kind, under any false or fraudulent Pretence . . . Every Person having in his or her Custody or Possession any Picklock Key, Crow, Jack, Bit or other Implement, with intent feloniously to break into any Dwellinghouse, Warehouse, Coach House, Stable or Outbuilding, or being armed with any Gun, Pistol, Hanger, Cutlass, Bludgeon, or other offensive weapon, or having upon him or her any Instrument with intent to commit any felonious Act; every Person being found in or upon any Dwelling-house . . ." and so on and so on. It was a long catalogue of malefactors, and it embraced, all too tightly, the Spiritualistic medium, who was to be as cardinal to his persuasion as usually a beneficed clergyman was to his. It must not be forgotten that the Vagrancy Act became law at least a quarter of a century before Spiritualism began to be practised in this country, but because witchcraft and Spiritualism were regarded as synonymous the old statute was applied to the new situation.

Neither the Witchcraft Act nor the Vagrancy Act were dead letters so far as they affected Spiritualists. Even outside the law court it was common to bracket witchcraft and Spiritualism. When Professor William Barrett, for instance, tried to bring Spiritualistic phenomena before the British Association for the Advancement of Science in 1876 the Biological Committee refused to hear him, and referred his paper to the Anthropological Sub-section who called upon their chairman, Dr. Alfred Russel Wallace, to exercise his casting vote before agreeing to listen to Barrett's address. During this debate one member asked why, since they had discussed ancient witchcraft the year before, they should not examine modern witchcraft at their current meeting? This attitude persisted as late as 1929, for when Mr. C. L'Estrange Ewen published his *Witch Hunting and Witch Trials* that year he offset the charge of superstitious bigotry levelled against the witch hunters and their dupes with a similar charge against Spiritualists.

"So at the present time," Mr. Ewen wrote, "in our equally superstitious age the mediums, or the familiars or spirits which they summon, have never been able to accomplish any physical act outside the powers of some human being, or to attain to any mental achievement beyond the capacity of some living person. . . .That there is now as much superstition as in the past is clear from our religious rites, our belief in mascots, our dabbling in the occult, and our attempts to receive the idle chatter of ghosts, and ascribing the manifestations of natural phenomena, coupled with legerdemain and trickery, to the restlessness of departed spirits.

"To be honest, we of the present generation can offer little adverse criticism of the witchcraft believers. In the future, among a more enlightened people, with more exact scientific observation and inference and knowledge of fundamental factors, no doubt the ancient witch-mania will be classed equally with the present spiritualistic phantasmagoria and charlatancy and religious rites and miraculous mumbo-jumbo, as the products of an exceedingly ignorant, gullible and superstitious age."

No sign of Mr. Ewen's militant scepticism was apparent in the House of Commons' debate on the Fraudulent Mediums Bill when the Second Reading began on December 1, 1950. The members who spoke included Churchmen, Unitarians, Congregationalists, Methodists, Roman Catholics, Jews, convinced Spiritualists and those who said firmly that after investigation they remained unconvinced. No member attacked Spiritualism as a fraud or a pretence. The few who spoke against the Bill did so on legalistic grounds. Most speakers welcomed the measure as a means of removing an injustice and of extending religious liberty. Although it was a Private Member's Bill, the Home Office had co-operated in its drafting, and the Home Secretary, Mr. Chuter Ede, made one of the most effective speeches in its support. No group in the House placed obstacles in the way of its passing. Spiritualism indeed was given Parliament's blessing, and within six months of its introduction the Bill became law.

It is instructive to read the record of the debate on the Bill as it is reported in *Hansard*. The very unanimity of the members is significant in view of the fierceness of the opposition Spiritualism had hitherto aroused. Indeed it is in some ways regrettable that the case against Spiritualism was not put before Parliament and allowed to go by default. For there is an opposition case. The Roman Catholic Church is uncompromisingly against Spiritualism and its practices, and even outside that body there are many distinguished thinkers who hold that Spiritualism is a chimera. One would have liked to have heard their voice.

Nevertheless there were some members, such as the Rev. Gordon Lang, M.P. for Stalybridge and Hyde, who, while supporting the Bill, testified that they remained unconvinced of the Spiritualists' contention. Mr. Lang amused the House by confiding to them that the only time he had gazed into a crystal he saw things from the past which he would rather not have seen, and nothing at all about the future. And he added that before the 1931 Election Sir Arthur Conan Doyle had written him a letter, which he still possessed, and in it Sir Arthur had said the spirit world would look after Mr. Lang and that he need not worry about the next election or any other election. "Unfortunately," Mr. Lang continued, "his friends were not on the Register of Electors, or it may be that, as I was a young and innocent lad at the time, they thought it would be better that I should be spared from this House for some time. At any rate, at the subsequent election I had the heaviest defeat that I have ever received." Such an experience might well have aroused a prejudice against Spiritualists and their assertions. But not in Mr. Lang. He said that he gladly supported the Bill. Again, Mr. Gibson, M.P. for Clapham, told the House that he had read everything written by Sir Oliver Lodge concerning Spiritualism and had not been persuaded by it. Similarly, he had read everything Mr. Hannen Swaffer had written on the subject, and still he was not persuaded. Even so, he supported the Bill on the general principle that there ought to be complete freedom to express

one's thought, to preach one's philosophy, and to try to persuade others to accept it in whatever way one feels that can
best be done, so long as it does not take away from others the
right also to express their point of view. Mr. Mellish, M.P.
for Bermondsey, confessed that, because of his religious faith, he
had never attended a Spiritualist meeting; indeed, his religion
laid it down that he should not do so. "Of one thing I am
certain," Mr. Mellish continued, "and that is that the principle
of all Christian faith is the belief in an after life. I think that is
demonstrated by all Christians, whether they are Protestants or
Catholics or whatever they may be. They believe there is
another life. Those who believe in Spiritualism believe that they
can have contact with those who are in that other life. I have
no right to criticise those people, because I do not know. If I
want to find out, it is up to me to go to one of their meetings
and find out for myself." He, too, supported the Bill.

Mr. Monslow, M.P. for Barrow-in-Furness, who introduced
the Bill, gave an account of the present strength of the
Spiritualist movement. There are 1,000 churches, he said,
affiliated into two main organisations, the Spiritualists
National Union and the Greater World Christian Spiritualist
League. Mr. Monslow said that the active membership of
these bodies was 50,000. "In addition," he went on, "there
are thousands of adherents who attend Spiritualist services
but who are not actual members of the Spiritualist Church.

"The Spiritualist movement is not only a movement which
operates in Britain, but is a world-wide one, recognized by
the State in many countries. At the international conference
held in London in 1948, forty-one countries were represented."

Mr. Rogers, M.P. for Kensington North, quoted the result
of an inquiry which, he said, had been conducted by Mass
Observation in January 1947. This showed, he said, "that 35
out of every 100 people contacted in their inquiry believed in
Spiritualism—a very substantial number; 36 per cent believed
in ghosts; 51 per cent in second sight—that is, clairvoyance;
64 per cent in intuition, and 86 per cent in telepathy. There is
obviously an enormous number of people who do believe that

there is some validity in the claims of the Spiritualists to be able to demonstrate the validity of the after life". Though it is possible to question whether the Mass Observation sample is completely reliable for statistical estimates concerning national opinion as a whole, yet these figures and those of Mr. Monslow do suggest that the strength of the Spiritualist movement today is something to be reckoned with.

One important point put to the House by Lieutenant-Commander Thompson, M.P. for Croydon West, was this: It had taken 215 years from the passing of the Witchcraft Act of 1735, he said, "for us to realise the reality of what has been called, in one of those hateful, long, and involved phrases, extra-sensory perception.

"If the House gives a Second Reading to the Bill I shall welcome it not only because it removes from Spiritualists the stigma of prosecution under the old Vagrancy Act—I agree that that is necessary—but because it will also reaffirm that we honestly admit that there are powers given to some people in the community which enable them to do things which, for 215 years, we have not believed were physically possible."

Thus it came about that the Witchcraft Act, 1735, was repealed, and section 4 of the Vagrancy Act 1824, "so far as it extended to persons purporting to act as spiritualistic mediums or to exercise any powers of telepathy, clairvoyance, or other similar powers, or to persons who, in purporting so to act or to exercise such powers, use fraudulent devices". Instead, it was laid down that for an offence to be committed under the new Act there must be intent to deceive, or a fraudulent device used, with the object of obtaining reward. It was also stipulated that no proceedings for an offence under the Act could be brought in England and Wales without the consent of the Director of Public Prosecutions, and that nothing in the Act should apply to anything done solely for entertainment.

All sincere Spiritualists now had the protection of the law, and only the charlatan, the fake, and the parasite was liable to punishment. Spiritualism had attained a new status. For the first time in this country it had become respectable.

CHAPTER II

FROM CROOKES TO DOWDING

ODERN Spiritualism in this country begins with the
arrival at Southampton of Mrs. Hayden, an American
medium, in 1852. She was the wife of the editor of a
Boston newspaper. On her return home a year later she
studied medicine and afterwards practised as a doctor. Mrs.
Hayden was, therefore, a woman of some social and intellectual
pretensions. In London she took rooms in Queen Anne
Street, where, so she advertised, "spiritual phenomena would
be forthcoming from 12—3 p.m. and from 4—6 p.m. daily".
She was also willing to visit her patrons in their own homes
and for this service her charge was £1 1s. a head.

Mrs. Hayden was quickly accepted by Victorian society,
and her pioneering work aroused lively interest, not all of it
favourable. She made many converts, of whom the most distinguished was Robert Owen, of New Lanark, an industrialist
whose niche in economic history, at least, is secure. She was,
however, criticised by W. G. Wills in Charles Dickens's magazine *Household Words,* and an even more formidable onslaught came from George Henry Lewes, the philosopher
and husband of George Eliot. Against these attacks she
was defended by Professor Augustus De Morgan, the
mathematician.

Mrs. Hayden impressed most of her sitters as an intelligent,
attractive young woman, patient, good-tempered, artless, and
simple and candid in her manners. Thus equipped, her tour
was, on the whole, successful. Lady Combermere arranged
the first of her seances for her, and presently the London
hostesses were pressing for her to demonstrate for them and
their guests. "In those days," it was said, "you were invited
to Tea and Table Moving as a new excitement."

To a later generation, accustomed to the work of many and varied mediums, Mrs. Hayden's powers must seem sharply limited. She sought no other means of communicating with the dead than by means of spirit raps. Those raps were once described by Professor De Morgan as "a hailstorm of knitting-needles". To her sitters she gave a printed alphabet, a pencil, and a piece of paper. They were told to note each letter at which they heard a distinct rap. In this way whole, coherent, and meaningful sentences were communicated. The technique was simple; the results, so many of her sitters testified, impressive.

The furore occasioned by Mrs. Hayden encouraged other Spiritualists from America to cross the Atlantic, and homespun mediums also came forward. Michael Faraday, who had achieved so much in the field of electricity, was inspired to test this plethora of spirit raps, and for this purpose he designed special apparatus. Faraday's conclusion was that the raps were simply the result of unconscious muscular action on the part of the sitter. This dampened the early ardour aroused by the attractive Mrs. Hayden, and there was a steep decline in interest until the glamorous, the extraordinary, and the enigmatic Daniel Douglas Home landed at Liverpool on April 9, 1855.

Home, who had been born at Currie, near Edinburgh, in 1833, had been taken to America when nine years of age by the aunt who adopted him. During his boyhood he appeared to display a certain psychic capacity which strengthened during his adolescence. His aunt fancied that he was in league with the devil, and in the end she drove him from her house. But throughout his career Home never lacked friends and he had at hand those who would support him. It is not to be questioned that he must have exercised unusual personal magnetism which few people were able to resist. Robert Browning was certainly able to, but then he fancied he had been injured by it, for he was jealous of the hold that Home seemed in his eyes to have over his wife, Elizabeth Barrett Browning. This ability to win friends whenever he needed them enabled Home, with little means and shot through with tuberculosis, never to go without the comforts of life, for it is to his credit that he refused to accept fees for his sittings. "I have been sent on a mission," he said. "That mission is to demonstrate immortality. I have never taken money for it and I never will." A personal gift of jewellery from a prince or a duke was another matter. But money, no. The handsome, elegant, emaciated young man was much too fastidious for that.

Home's charm of manner combined with the quality of his mediumship made his company eagerly sought by a wide variety of people. He used to say that he would never refuse to hold a seance if by so doing there was a possibility of his advancing the cause of Spiritualism, and it is a fact that he seldom left a house without having made both converts and friends. He was able to live in comfortable rooms in the West End of London. His conversation is said always to have been impeccable. So high was the tone of religious morality which appeared to pervade him that it effectively checked all approach to light talk on the part of those who associated with him. At least that is the testimony of Sir William Crookes, the scientist, who added that so far as Home's character was concerned he thoroughly believed in his uprightness and honour. Crookes believed that Home was incapable of practising deception or meanness.

In Europe Home's patrons were drawn largely from the ranks of those whose names were recorded in Burke's *Peerage* and the *Almanach de Gotha*. Among his London sitters were Lord Brougham, the Earl of Dunraven, Lord Paget, Lord Adare, Lord Lindsay, the Duchess of Sutherland, Lady Shelley, and Lady Otway. When he crossed the English Channel kings and princes commanded him to demonstrate before them. He became the friend of the Empress Eugenie, who argued that his demonstrations could not possibly be impostures because no one would dare to deceive her and Napoleon III. Tsar Alexander of Russia sponsored Home's marriage, and he sat with Wilhelm I of Prussia, and the Kings of Bavaria and Württemberg. Home's powers did not stop short at spirit rappings but extended to the levitation of objects and even of himself, for he would float in the air feet first and pass from side to side of a room. Sitters who said that his phenomena could not possibly have been impostures included Ruskin, Thackeray, John Bright, Lord Dufferin, Sir Edwin Arnold, and Nassau Senior—a distinguished company. Towards the end of his life—he was fifty-three when he died—he seemed to have exhausted his psychic powers. He joined the Roman Catholic Church and was persuaded by his confessor that his gifts were of the devil. He thought of joining a monastic order, but after the lapse of a year his mediumship returned to him with all its force.

Sir Arthur Conan Doyle has called Home "the greatest physical medium the modern world has seen". A more critical investigator, Whately Carington, has written that Home was "almost unique not only as a classical example of a physical medium but as never having been exposed in imposture, or even at all convincingly accused of it". This is an overstatement. Robert Browning was firmly convinced that he had detected Home in a fraudulent act, and there was a similar incident in Paris which led Dr. Berthez to write: "Mr. Home, aware that his tricks have been found out, cuts a wretched figure." Sir William Crookes, who conducted a series of test sittings with Home during his investigation of Spiritualism, was indecisive in his opinion of the medium's powers. "The experiments I have tried have been very numerous," Crookes finally reported, "but owing to our imperfect knowledge of the conditions which favour or oppose the manifestations of this force, to the apparently capricious manner in which it is exerted, and to the fact that Mr. Home himself is subject to unaccountable ebbs and flows of the force, it has but seldom happened that a result obtained on one occasion could be subsequently confirmed and tested with apparatus specially contrived for the purpose."

Crookes has left lengthy accounts of his seances with Home, who specially impressed him by refusing to sit in the dark if it could be avoided. Sometimes the sittings were violent, for chairs were knocked about, the table floated six inches off the floor and then dashed down, and raucous noises were heard. One member of the circle was lifted high in the air, floated across the room, and then dropped with a crash of pictures and ornaments at the far side of the room. Crookes's brother tried to keep hold of one of the floater's hands, but it was torn from his grasp as he passed above the table. Then an accordion rose from the table and travelled round the room playing all the while accompanied by a man's fine voice. Sometimes the accordion seemed to be in two places at once, so quickly did it travel. During the sitting seven distinct spirit voices were heard. A hand was seen without arm or body attached to it. Most of the sitters said they felt other hands stroking their faces. Home's handkerchief was gently laid on the heads, shoulders, and hands of those in the circle, and was then carried elsewhere. "I feel it impossible to describe to you all the striking things that took place, or to convey the intense feeling of genuineness and reality which they caused in our minds," Crookes wrote to his friend, Dr. Huggins, a Fellow of the Royal Society, "but I want you to come and attend at another seance which is appointed for next Tuesday week, the 25th inst., at Russell Square, when Home has promised to come, and we are going to get the same party and if possible the same conditions. You must, however, prepare for the chance of a failure. Home was in wonderful power last night, but he is the most uncertain of mediums, and it is quite as likely that the next time absolutely nothing will take place."

Dr. E. E. Fournier D'Albe, in his *Life of Sir William Crookes*, has pointed out that two of those taking part in the seance thus described were later convicted of fraud. Home, it is true, was not one of these, but the phenomena that so excited Crookes were, in his biographer's opinion, absolutely devoid of evidential value. The two who had thus become suspect were not present, however, at another seance which took place on May 31, 1871, in Crookes's house in Mornington Road. Dr. Huggins was present and so was Crookes's chemical assistant, Gimingham. Elaborate precautions were taken and Crookes introduced apparatus of his own. Whenever anything of importance was experienced during the demonstration Crookes and his sister-in-law kept their feet on those of Home. Loud raps were heard. A gust of cold air was felt, though the temperature of the room was above 70 degrees. Gimingham felt a touch and his chair move slightly. A message, spelled out by raps, read, "I will do it again, you dear old Chinchilla." The last word naturally caused some mystification and was amended, by means of raps, to "Rosa Gill". An accordion held by Home was taken from him by some unseen agency and floated about the room while playing *Home, Sweet Home*. Other messages were received, and more phenomena observed which deeply impressed Crookes, who in the autumn of that year conducted a series of seances with another American medium, Katie Fox, and yet a third series, now among the classics of Spiritualism, with Florence Cook of Hackney.

Unlike Crookes, Robert Browning was so outraged by Home that he took him for the prototype of *Mr. Sludge, 'The Medium'*. His wife, Elizabeth Barrett Browning, on the other hand, held unwavering belief in the genuineness of Home's powers. Browning's detestation of Home arose out of a seance he attended with Elizabeth at Ealing. Browning thought that Home was fraudulently using his feet to produce phenomena and stumped out of the seance, taking his wife with him. "What chiefly went against Robert's mind," Elizabeth wrote to her sister, "was the trance at the conclusion, during which the medium talked a great deal of twaddle as may be heard in any fifth-rate conventicle. . . . For my part I am confirmed in all my opinions. To me it was wonderful and conclusive, and I believe that the medium present was no more responsible for the things said than I was myself."

When *Mr. Sludge, 'The Medium'* was published, Home reviewed it in the *Spiritualist Magazine* for July 1864 and gave this account of the incident: Before the Brownings arrived for the seance the children of the house had been gathering

flowers and these were made into a wreath of clematis. Somehow this wreath came to be placed on the table in the seance
room. "During the seance," Home continues, "it was raised
from the table by supernatural power in the presence of us all
and while we were watching it." Browning was standing
behind his wife. The wreath passed slowly to Mrs. Browning
and was placed on her head. In Home's opinion Browning
was upset because this compliment of being crowned poet
went to his wife and not to him. Browning's reply, in a letter
to Mrs. W. B. Kinney dated January 6, 1871, was to dismiss
Home's version of the seance as "a vomit of lies", and to call
the medium "an unmitigated scoundrel". The letter goes on:
"If I ever cross the fellow's path I shall probably be silly
enough to soil my shoe by kicking him—but I should prefer
keeping that disgrace from myself as long as possible. Indeed,
I have got to consider such a beast as the proper associate and
punishment of those who choose to shut their eyes and open
their arms to bestiality incarnate."

Such was the mood in which Browning composed *Mr.
Sludge, 'The Medium'*. The name has stuck, to the disrepute
of mediumship in general. This poem in blank verse is a
remorseless exposure of a man who is a cheat, a liar, and a
hypocrite. It is certain that Browning's attack would have
carried little weight if he had presented no more than a
portrait of an unredeemed villain; a character so black would
not have convinced those sophisticated readers who find their
pleasure in poetry. Browning, however, was too able a literary
artist thus to have been led artistically astray even in his anger,
and he puts into the mouth of Sludge so plausible a defence
that, in various adapted forms, it is still offered today to excuse
the impostures of mediums who have been discovered in fraud.
The whining Sludge begins with a wheedling plea to be let off:

> *Now don't, sir! don't expose me just this once!*
> *This was the first and only time, I'll swear—*
> *Look at me—see, I kneel—the only time*
> *I swear I ever cheated—yes, by the soul*

Of Her who hears (your sainted Mother, sir!)
All, except this last accident, was truth—
This little kind of slip!—and even this
It was your own wine, sir, the good champagne,
(I took it for Catawba, you're so kind)
Which put this folly in my head.

Sludge then turns and seeks to blame his patron for encouraging him in his folly. "It's a conceit of yours that ghosts may be," he tells his benefactor, and goes on to say of mediumship that

It's fancying, fable-making, nonsense work—
What never meant to be so very bad—
The knack of story-telling, brightening up
Each dull old bit of fact that drops its shine.
One does see somewhat when one shuts one's eyes,
If only spots and streaks; tables do tip
In the oddest way of themselves: and pens, good Lord,
Who knows if you drive them or they drive you?

But presently he drops these sophistries and describes the temptation that faces a poor boy when, within a week of being acclaimed a medium, able to communicate with the world of spirit, he finds himself

Sweet and clean, dining daintily, dizened smart,
Set on a stool buttressed by ladies' knees,
Each soft smiler calling me her pet,
Encouraging her story to uncoil
And creep out from its hole inch after inch.

That temptation is real and potent. Every fashionable medium is open to it. The acclaim he receives, the money and the presents that are showered upon him, and the sense of power that comes with success lead him on, unless his character is of the strongest, to overwork and exhaust his power. It is all too hard to let fame and fortune slip away. He becomes obsessed with the notion that he must satisfy all his clients all the time, and so if results do not come he may begin to fake them. One of the most reputable of all mediums, Mrs. Osborne Leonard, who acted for Sir Arthur Conan Doyle, refused to take more than two clients in a day. "It is to this, no doubt, that the sustained excellence of her results are due," Sir Arthur wrote. And another great medium, Alderman Evan Powell, of Paignton, who has sat with millionaires and princes without the slightest breath of criticism ever fanning upon him, adopted a similar iron principle. "Evan Powell may be said to have the widest endowment of spiritual gifts of any medium at present in England," Sir Arthur Conan Doyle wrote in 1926 in his *History of Spiritualism*. "He preaches the doctrines of Spiritualism both in his own person and while under control, and he can in himself exhibit nearly the whole range of phenomena. It is a pity that his business as a coal merchant in Devonshire prevents his constant presence in London."

Which course did Home take? We shall never know the truth. Sir William Crookes, for all his scientific training, never detected him in an imposture. Whatever Browning and the French doctor may have believed, however much rumour may have buzzed about his name, Home was never *publicly* exposed. Not one of his detractors ever pressed a charge against him concerning his mediumship in a court of law or before an investigating committee. Nevertheless it may be significant that at one period Home did exhaust his powers completely. After a year's rest they returned to him. In some respects his character was unstable: that is at least suggested by the way in which he flitted from one religious creed to another. We know that, apart from his mediumship, he had no means of making a living, and though he charged no fees for his seances yet these did provide him with an entry into a life of considerable luxury. Did he fake his results when he found his capacities waning? Was he, indeed, the utter fraud that Browning represented him to be? We have no means of knowing, and must decide these problems according to our own individual judgments. But these questions have more than academic importance. Thus early in the history of British Spiritualism a controversy was stirred up. Its arguments were to be repeated in almost identical terms by succeeding generations concerning later mediums. An atmosphere of doubt was generated that has never been entirely dispelled, and a suggestion of chicanery imparted that Spiritualism has never been able completely to erase.

All the same, Spiritualists have tried, by pointing to the weighty reputations of so many of their adherents, to combat the damage that is done to their movement whenever one of their number is exposed in an imposture. It is not strictly accurate to say, as Sir Oliver Lodge once did when writing in the *Encyclopaedia Britannica,* that "Spiritualists have, as a rule, sought to convince not by testimony but by ocular demonstration". They have often tried, and still do try, to establish conviction in their creed by exhibiting the achievements, in other fields, of the most distinguished of their adherents. And rightly so. Sir Oliver Lodge himself was one such instance. Sir Arthur Conan Doyle another. Sir Edward Marshall Hall, the advocate, a third. These men were not fools, the defenders of Spiritualism insist. They were men of probity. They had been trained all their lives to sift evidence whether in science, in law, or in literature. Were they to be hoodwinked, the rhetorical question is asked, by the performances of masquerading conjurors? And of these champions the first, and by no means least, was Sir William Crookes, the physicist.

There is no gainsaying Crookes's eminence as a scientist. His discoveries speak for that. It was he who isolated thallium and a new element in gadolinite. He invented the spinthariscope, the Crookes' Tube, and a gas-filled X-ray tube. He was a fellow of the Royal Society and before his death in 1919 he received the highest of Civil Honours, the Order of Merit. This, then, was the man, of first-rate intellect and critical ability, who began to make researches into psychic phenomena in 1870 because he thought that all the so-called manifesta-

B

tions might prove to be a trick. He ended by becoming convinced of their authenticity, siding with other great scientists such as A. R. Wallace, Darwin's fellow worker, Lord Rayleigh, Sir Oliver Lodge, and Sir William Barrett, though they have all been severely criticised for alleged weaknesses in their experimental technique. Even so, when Crookes presided at the British Association meeting at Bristol in 1898 he said boldly: "No incident in my scientific career is more widely known than the part I took many years ago in certain psychic researches. Thirty years have passed since I published an account of experiments tending to show that outside our scientific knowledge there exists a Force exercised by intelligence differing from the ordinary intelligence common to mortals. . . . I have nothing to retract. I adhere to my already published statements. Indeed, I might add much thereto." Some years later he said he believed it to be true "that a connexion has been set up between this world and the next". He thought, he said, that Spiritualism had killed the old materialism of the scientists, because "it has at least convinced the great majority of people, who know anything about the subject, of the existence of the next world".

Here Crookes was plainly touching one of the live nerves of Victorian England, the contest between those who were on the side of the apes and those who thought to range themselves with the angels. Spiritualism and the New Science were contemporaries. Charles Darwin, let it be remembered, published his *Origin of Species* in 1859 and *The Descent of Man* in 1871. It was these books which precipitated the bitter clash between Science and Religion. That was an age when to lose one's faith was a shattering experience. Tennyson might cry, "There lives more faith in honest doubt, believe me, than in half the creeds", but his contemporaries were not ready to listen to him. You believed, or you did not believe. The Victorians had no room for doubt, honest or otherwise. Not to believe was for most of them to be left naked to eternity. And here was the terrible Darwin apparently exposing as nonsense so much of the lore and parables of religion with his carefully observed and assembled facts. How could one believe in the truth of religion when he destroyed legends that men had been taught to regard as divinely-inspired narratives? Concurrently, however, Spiritualism was presenting another set of phenomena which, if true, must give rational authority to the doctrine of personal immortality, of which the possibility is among the greater spiritual comforts religion can offer. It was this dilemma that led Mr. Gladstone to say to F. W. H. Myers, soon after the foundation of the Society for Psychical Research, that the inquiry this organisation had set itself was "the most important work which is being done in the world. 'By far the most important,' he repeated with a grave emphasis which suggested previous trains of thought. . . . He . . . ended by saying: 'If you will accept sympathy without service, I shall be glad to join your ranks.' He became an Honorary Member and followed with attention . . . the successive issues of our *Proceedings*."

T. H. Huxley, the indomitable defender of Darwinism, had himself been brought up, he said, "in the strictest school of evangelical orthodoxy". Accordingly he had begun his career as a scientist with little doubt about the general truth of what he had been taught, only to turn in time from that faith to its opposite. He knew, therefore, the "unpleasantness of being called an 'infidel' ". The unpleasantness of that experience he underwent again and again, as did so many more independent thinkers among his contemporaries. He was, in the last analysis, a materialist. He never came to believe in the existence of a future life. He remained dissatisfied with the evidence that was offered him concerning the reality of the soul. Yet he did not revile those whose faith, he said, was more robust and whose hopes were richer than his. "I confess," he wrote, "that my dull moral sense does not enable me to see anything base or selfish in the desire for a future life among the spirits of the just made perfect; or even among such poor fallible souls as one has known here below."

One outcome of the wrangle between Science and Religion at that time was the birth of the Society for Psychical Research in 1882. It is still actively at work, as the next chapter will show. The Society was largely founded through the energy of three men, all of whom were associated with Trinity College, Cambridge. Of this triumvirate the leader was the classicist and moral philosopher, Henry Sidgwick, who turned to psychic research in 1859 while still an undergraduate because he believed that "direct proof of continual individual existence" was important if the accepted standards of morality were to prevail over an abandoned hedonism. Psychical research became one of the dominant interests of his life, intruding into his philosophical and theological work. He argued that the study of miracles demanded its investigation, and he further urged that the possibility of continued individual existence after death could not be neglected either from a theological or an ethical point of view. Sidgwick was not an orthodox Churchman, though he was most certainly no materialist. But his concern over the imposition of religious tests at the University inspired him to throw up his Trinity fellowship. He was president of the S.P.R. for the first three years of its existence and again from 1888 to 1893, but at the end he seems to have reached no definite conclusions concerning survival after death.

His two closest fellow workers in the field of psychic research were Edmund Gurney, musician and humanitarian, and Frederic W. H. Myers, poet, lecturer at Trinity College, and an inspector of schools under the Education Department, a post once filled by Matthew Arnold. Myers was one of those whose faith had been overthrown by the impact of the new science. He has left on record how, during a starlight walk with Henry Sidgwick on December 3, 1869, he asked the philosopher, "almost with trembling", whether he thought that when tradition, intuition, metaphysics had failed to solve the riddles that were so perplexing there was still a chance "that from any actual observable phenomena—ghosts, spirits, whatsoever there might be—some valid knowledge might be drawn as to a World Unseen". Sidgwick agreed he had thought this was possible. "Steadily, though in no sanguine fashion,"

Myers wrote, "he indicated some last grounds of hope: and from that night onwards I resolved to pursue this quest, if it might be, at his side."

The collaboration of Sidgwick, Gurney, and Myers produced not only the S.P.R. but two of the great classics of psychical research, *Phantasms of the Living,* largely the work of Edmund Gurney, and Myers's *Human Personality and Its Survival of Bodily Death.* Gurney may justly be said to have killed himself through his labours on *Phantasms of the Living,* because nervous exhaustion which followed its completion led him to take an overdose of drugs to cure his sleeplessness and he was found dead one morning in a Brighton hotel at the age of forty-one. Of Myers's *Human Personality* William James, the American psychologist, wrote that it was "the first attempt to consider the phenomena of hallucination, hypnotism, automatism, double personality, and mediumship as connected parts of one whole subject". An important feature of Myers's work was his concern to see that the S.P.R. in its investigations preserved the strictest impartiality and did not veer in the slightest degree towards the militant sceptics on the one side or the embattled believers on the other.

Two more men who helped to found the S.P.R. deserve to be mentioned here to show something of the quality of those early inquirers and the climate of their times. One is Richard Hodgson, a brilliant investigator who was able to apply his Indian experience to his task of criticism. The other was Frank Podmore, a Civil Servant employed in the Post Office, and one of the originators of the Fabian Society. Podmore began by accepting the tenet of spiritual survival after bodily death, only to declare later to the National Association of Spiritualists that he had become sceptical about Spiritualistic doctrine. Podmore wrote one of the earliest histories of Spiritualism. He was a member of the Council of the S.P.R. from 1882 until 1909, and he did not hesitate to criticise even Myers. Podmore believed that what were commonly regarded as psychical phenomena could be explained either by psychology or by telepathy instead of being accepted as communications from the spirit world. Other members and associates who were in at the birth of the S.P.R. were Arthur Balfour, later to be Prime Minister, his brother Gerald Balfour, William Bateson the rediscoverer of Mendelism, Lewis Carroll, Leslie Stephen, and John Ruskin.

The Society for Psychical Research has, however, never been a Spiritualistic body, though many and extremely distinguished Spiritualists have belonged to it. In this respect it has continued to be true to its original manifesto, which stated: "It has been widely felt that the present is an opportune time for making an organised and systematic attempt to investigate that large group of debatable phenomena designated by such terms as mesmeric, psychical, and Spiritualistic. . . . The aim of the Society will be to approach these various problems without prejudice or prepossession of any kind, and in the same spirit of exact and unimpassioned enquiry which has enabled science to solve so many problems, once not less obscure nor less hotly debated." Then comes this: "Note. To prevent misconception, it is here expressly stated that Membership of this Society does not imply the acceptance of any particular explanation of the phenomena investigated, nor any belief as to the operation, in the physical world, of forces other than those recognised by Physical Science."

Nevertheless the Rev. Stainton Moses, a graduate of Oxford and a member of the Church of England, could feel at ease among the members of the S.P.R., though he had been practising mediumship and automatic writing since 1872. Moses, a copious propagandist, was to write in *Spirit Teachings* what has come to be regarded as the "Bible" of Spiritualism. Again, the Castor and Pollux of latter-day Spiritualism, Sir Oliver Lodge and Sir Arthur Conan Doyle, were both leading members of the S.P.R., although near the end of his life Conan Doyle threw up his membership in disgust at its policy: it seemed to him to incline too much towards psychical scepticism for his ardent, believing soul. Yet the scrupulous objectivity with which the Society has always tried to carry out its inquiries has frequently served to buttress Spiritualism,

as, for example, when it has accepted the *bona fides* of some
novel and startling medium.

The embracing of Spiritualism by Lodge and Doyle gave
undoubtedly a great fillip to the movement, for they reflected
upon it some of their own illustrious prestige. There was no
denying Sir Oliver Lodge's scientific eminence. His is one of
the great names in the development of radio, and there were
other fields in which his authority was not to be challenged.
So, too, with Sir Arthur Conan Doyle. The creator of Sherlock
Holmes, Brigadier Gerard, The White Company, and Rodney
Stone was more than a popular storyteller: he was a shrewd
and penetrating sifter of evidence, as his defence of Oscar
Slater and Edalji showed. Such men as these were not to be
dismissed as sentimental old women, willing to swallow, as
signs and wonders, the crude tricks of conjurors posing as
mediums. Of equal standing was Edward Marshall Hall,
that almost fabulous advocate, who turned to Spiritualism,
so his biographer, Edward Marjoribanks, has written, in
the hope of discovering from it that in some way the bitter-
ness and unhappiness engendered in this life between those
who ought to be everything to each other would be redressed
and explained. "How utterly incomplete," Marshall Hall
wrote in one of his last letters, "would the best things in this
life be, if the grave were to be the end of all these things. I do
believe that our souls are immortal." Finally in our own day
we have seen a man whom we know to be a giant, Lord
Dowding, who led his few staunch hearts to victory in the
Battle of Britain, planning their strategy and husbanding their
strength, publicly proclaiming his conviction in the Spiritualistic doctrines that the soul survives the grave and that communication between this world and the next is possible. Nor is
he alone among men and women of eminence in holding those
beliefs. Among the honorary vice-presidents of the Marylebone Spiritualist Association are such people as Sir John
Anderson, Sir Charles Blackmore, Lieutenant-Colonel Angus
Davidson, Brigadier D. S. Davidson, the Rev. Sir Herbert
Dunnico, Brigadier R. C. Firebrace, Lady Beatrice Gore, Dr.

John Hettinger, Colonel R. Keyworth, Miss L. Lind-af Hageby, the Rev. George May, and Major-General Frank W. Ramsay. It is an imposing list, and it is by no means complete. Have they all been hoodwinked, deluded by fantastications? The rest of this book will seek to find an answer to that question, going in turn to the Spiritualists themselves, to the Churches, and to Science in the hope of elucidating what certain knowledge we now have, after a century of Spiritualism, of life beyond the grave, and the mental capacities and limitations of Man.

CHAPTER III

THE S.P.R. AND THE SCIENTISTS

THE library of the Society for Psychical Research at its headquarters in Tavistock Square, Bloomsbury, is a good place to retire to when one wishes to clarify one's thinking. Normally there are few people in the library. It is a spacious room and quiet, free of hurry and bustle. Its rows of books look down benignly from their shelves. The volumes deal, it is true, with extraordinary subjects, but the treatment they adopt is reassuringly matter-of-fact. One's feet seem always to be on firm ground. There is no hysteria in most of these pages, no abandonment to emotion. They generate a confident expectation in the reader that he is being led with patient assurance towards ultimate truth.

The Society's *Proceedings* have been published now for more than seventy years and fill many weighty volumes. These I thumbed through one afternoon with the object of comparing the changes that have taken place in the Society's studies, the shifts of emphasis, and the opening of new investigations since Sidgwick, Gurney, Myers, and their sympathisers set up this body in 1882. And so it was that I came across the story of Chaffin's will.

James L. Chaffin was a farmer in North Carolina who made a will in November 1905 leaving all his money to his eldest son. He revoked this will in 1919 without telling anyone he had done so, and directed that his estate was to be divided equally among his four children. The new will he placed in the family Bible, and he scribbled a note, "Read the twenty-seventh chapter of Genesis in my Daddy's old bible", which he sewed into an inside pocket of his overcoat. Why he should have acted in this way is not explained, but he was living, it must be understood, in a backward, rural community where behaviour ought not to be judged by urban, present-day conventions.

Chaffin died from an accident in 1921. His first will—no one knew of any other—was proved on September 24, 1921. In June 1925 J. P. Chaffin, the second of the sons, dreamed he saw his father wearing his black overcoat and that he heard him say: "You will find my will in my overcoat pocket." Accordingly, the son went to his mother's house and asked for the dead man's garment. He was told it had been given to one of his brothers who lived twenty miles away. So he went there and found the clue that his father had stitched into the pocket. He returned with witnesses to his mother's house and searched, as the note directed, for the family Bible. It was found in a bureau drawer in an upstairs-room. The Bible was so old and decayed that it came apart as soon as it was examined. But inside it was the will.

The brother who had proved the first will and inherited old Chaffin's estate had died, leaving a widow and a young son. The second will was offered for probate and the case was brought to trial. Ten witnesses came forward to testify that the second will was in James L. Chaffin's handwriting. Once this document was shown to the widow and her son they admitted its genuineness. The court therefore rescinded the first will and substituted the later one. "It is hard to suggest a satisfactory explanation of the facts on normal lines," comments the S.P.R. in its report on this extraordinary instance of what appears to be the clairvoyant communication of an apparition unassociated with a crisis.

When in 1882 the S.P.R. divided itself into working committees one of the subjects allotted for investigation was thus defined: "(4) A careful investigation of any reports, resting on strong testimony, regarding apparitions at the moment of death, or otherwise, or regarding disturbances in houses reputed to be haunted." Thus it was that nearly half a century later the story of the American farmer's testimentary precautions came within the purview of the Society.

In all ages dreams have aroused the interest of mankind, but never have they been so studied and pondered over as in our own times. Freud and the psycho-analysts have invested them with therapeutic importance, and J. W. Dunne, believing that dreams can have prophetic significance, attempted to build on them a metaphysical system, though his theories—apart from his facts—have been ridiculed by philosophers.

More recently Mrs. Louisa Rhine, the wife of Professor J. B. Rhine, the psychologist, of Duke University, U.S.A., has collected 1,600 instances of dreamlike forebodings from people in many parts of the world, and these reports she has attempted to analyse and classify statistically for the benefit of later students. Her task has been a difficult one, for into what pigeon-hole should such an experience as this be put:

"Last July my uncle was lying fully awake in bed when he says he saw his eldest son standing by the bed, who told him, 'Well, Dad, you will have to take care of the children now.' This occurred a short time before the radio reported that one of the three bombers on a round-the-world trip had crashed off the coast of Persia. Later they established the fact that it was the one in which his son was the co-pilot. He was the father of four small children."

Actually, Mrs. Rhine lists that instance with the apparitional type of Dramatic Visions. Other variations are the Symbolic and the Photographic. She has also classified her collection of dreams under the headings of Foreknowledge, Telepathy, Clairvoyance, and Psychokinesis—those having a physical effect. Out of her batch, 539 visions reported foreknowledge of an event that took place later, 188 suggested telepathy, and 663 were undifferentiated. The dreams or forebodings have also been grouped according to whether they were experienced asleep or awake. Mrs. Rhine's survey leads her to think that people are more often convinced of the truth of these psychic experiences when they come to them in a waking state than if they are "seen" when asleep.

"What determines these limitations?" Mrs. Rhine asks. "Why does the threshold permit the passage of conviction in one case, inhibit it in another? Or why is the essential meaning transmitted in some cases, repressed in others?

"Are these limitations based on personality characteristics? If so, what kind? And what control can the subject or the experimenter exercise when these questions are answered?" To learn the answers, research will go on.

The study of dreams, however, was only a small part of the work to which the Society for Psychical Research set its hand at its inauguration. Five additional committees were set up, each charged with one of these tasks:

"An examination of the nature and extent of any influence which may be exerted by one mind upon another, apart from any generally recognised mode of perception.

"The study of hypnotism, and the forms of so-called mesmeric trance, with its alleged insensibility to pain; clairvoyance, and other allied phenomena.

"A critical revision of Reichenbach's researches with certain organisations called 'sensitives', and an enquiry whether such organisations possess any power of perception beyond a highly exalted sensibility of the recognised sensory organs.

"An enquiry into the various physical phenomena commonly called Spiritualistic; with an attempt to discover their causes and general laws.

"The collection and collation of existing materials bearing on the history of these subjects."

It is natural that since 1882 there have been striking changes and shifts of emphasis in the Society's work. So much, indeed, has been learned that matters which were suspect seventy years ago are now accepted unquestioningly as commonplaces, and lines of investigation that once seemed promising have been abandoned as fruitless.

Hypnotism, for example, was still regarded a century ago except by a few rare spirits as so much quackery. Sidgwick and his colleagues, however, were quick to accept the value placed upon hypnotism by such researchers as Braid, Esdaile, and Elliotson, and to see how this branch of applied psychology could be used for studying the structure of human personality, since there seemed to be grounds for believing that a hypnotised subject has extended powers of perception or cognition. Hypnotism had begun, under the German physician, F. A. Mesmer (1733-1815), as an extraordinary hotchpotch of humbug, quackery, and embryonic science. By the time of Mesmer's death his so-called discovery appeared to have been completely discredited. Then about 1841 it was resuscitated, in a severely disciplined and cleaned-up form, by James Braid, a Manchester doctor. When, a little later, Harriet Martineau, the Victorian blue-stocking, who was suffering from a malady that her doctors described as incurable, was restored by means of it to full health, it received a tremendous impetus.

Miss Martineau had been travelling on the Continent in 1839, when she fell seriously ill. She was found to be suffering from a tumour causing the enlargement and displacement of "an important organ". This condition was attended by acute internal pain and frequent weakening haemorrhages. Somehow she managed to struggle home to Tynemouth, special travelling devices being devised for her. Once home she was bed-fast, and so severe was the pain she suffered that her doctors had to drug her regularly. For two years she ate little food because of her perpetual sickness. Sir Charles Clarke, a medical specialist, ordered her to take three grains of iodide of iron daily, though he confessed he had prescribed iodine in an infinite number of cases without any benefit following. For three years Harriet Martineau likewise received no help from the treatment given her. Then in June 1844 she was persuaded to allow Spencer Hall, a wandering hypnotist who was demonstrating at that time in Newcastle, to see her. He treated her on two successive days, and on the third, when he was unable to attend, Miss Martineau's maid tried to see if she could copy his methods. Within three or four minutes, so Miss Martineau wrote afterwards, "delicious sensation of ease spread through me in a cool comfort before which all pain and distress gave way, oozing out, as it were, at the soles of my feet. During that hour and almost the whole evening I could no more help exclaiming with pleasure than can a person in torture crying out with pain. I became hungry and ate with relish for the first time for five years." By the beginning of December she had so far recovered that she was able to leave Tynemouth on a round of visits. She published an account of her experience, attributing her cure entirely to hypnotism. The furore this occasioned compelled her to give up her home and settle in the solitudes of the Lake District to escape the crowds who besieged her. Hypnotism had been popularly accepted.

Today hypnotism is commonly used in psychiatric practice. It has been stripped of all its former mumbo-jumbo and apparently magical qualities and turned into a recognised curative aid. Sometimes, however, it is exploited as a music-hall trick, the occasional dangers of which are beginning to arouse a certain amount of newspaper and political agitation. It has even been administered to dental patients and to women in labour, enabling them to bear their children without pain. The hypnotist does not need to be a Svengali or possessed of supernatural powers. There is reason to think that any normal person can practise it successfully provided he is given the complete co-operation of his subject. A high level of intelligence in the patient makes for easy hypnosis, because those thus gifted are able to assume the mental state of relaxed concentration which is the threshold to the trance condition when the hypnotist implants his healing suggestions —and other suggestions too if he so chooses. In that lies the danger of hypnotic practice—so it is commonly thought. By way of contrast, immature intellects, children, and animals are relatively difficult to hypnotise. If the subject resists the hypnotist it may take fifteen sittings to induce a trance. The psychiatrist is able to use the entranced state of the patient to remove certain phobias, doubts, or worries that are at the root of his trouble. In the wrong hands, however, a trance may be used for practical joking and even for worse things, though it is stated that no hypnotised person can be made to perform acts which he believes to be morally wrong, for then other layers of the will take control. I have seen an active young woman go repeatedly into a trance whenever the hypnotist snapped his fingers,—the sign she had been taught to associate with sleep. She stood fast asleep over a gas stove and could not be roused by any amount of shaking; she became completely entranced at the same signal while drinking a cup of tea; and on leaving the room she stood transfixed with her hand on the door-knob from which she could not move until the agreed command was made by the hypnotist. I have myself practised hypnotism—once, and once only. Duty took me to a demonstration arranged for the Press by an American who had been advising in the production of a film in which the story turned on the use of hypnotism. Some forty or fifty newspaper reporters were present. The demonstrator assured us that we could all, if we wished, be hypnotists, and he called for volunteers to test his technique. I was one of those who offered and presently a girl from another newspaper agreed to act as the subject. I am sure we were both entirely sceptical. But presently as I imitated the demonstrator's methods I had the girl deeply entranced. I suggested to her that she would feel no pain if I pricked her forearms, which were bare, with a pin. This I did repeatedly, and others in the room did so too. Visible scratches were left on her skin. She gave no sign, but slept on undisturbed. When she was awakened she vigorously denied she had ever been hypnotised and was both surprised and indignant to find she had been scratched—marks she was wholly unable to account for. I had that experience about ten years ago, and have never repeated it, partly because I have not been able to find a subject who would co-operate to the same extent. . . .

A similar change has taken place in the general attitude to the subject of telepathy. It is startling, when one knows something of the literature of this subject, to read this statement in Mr. H. Arthur Smith's presidential address to the S.P.R. in 1910: "'Telepathy' was a word unknown in our language until about five and twenty years ago." Nowadays, thanks largely to the clinching researches of Whately Carington, telepathy is accepted as a matter of course by the majority of those informed on the subject. Whately

Carington experimented with about 1,200 men and women living in Cambridge, Oxford, Edinburgh, Glasgow, Bristol, and Reading. The result of his strictly controlled and repeatable experiments showed that there is reason to believe that telepathy is an extra-sensory faculty shared by most people and perhaps by everyone. No one seems to possess this faculty at all strongly nor to be able to control it at will, but, all the same, it does undoubtedly seem to be present.

Six years after its foundation the Society for Psychical Research conducted a Census of Hallucinations which anticipated to some extent Mrs. Rhine's recent inquiry into dreams already referred to, for the question the Society put, and to which 17,000 answers were obtained, was this: "Have you ever, when believing yourself to be completely awake, had a vivid impression of seeing or being touched by a living or inanimate object, or of hearing a voice; which impression, so far as you can discover, was not due to any external physical cause?"

Until about 1926 the attention of the S.P.R., as shown by its *Proceedings*, was largely concentrated on the work of various mediums. The mediumship of Mrs. Piper, Willi Schneider, George Valiantine, Mrs. Osborne Leonard, and "Margery" was studied exhaustively by the members. In 1926, however, Dr. Hans Driesch sounded a new note in his presidential address. "Psychical research," he said, "will form the centre of all science and all philosophy, the very foundation of what we call in German *Weltanschauung*. At the present day the main need is to get psychical research under the strict control of experiment."

Almost immediately the Rhines came forward to meet this need with an experimental technique that was uncompromisingly scientific. They spent many years patiently testing, by means of special packs of cards and dice-throwing apparatus, the ability of their students, children, the blind, people in self-induced trances and others who were drugged or hypnotised, to foretell the future or practise clairvoyance. After a generation of fierce controversy the Rhines' methods were generally agreed to be sound and their conclusions have won wide acceptance. In 1948 Professor Rhine was able to pose, and answer, this question: "Is there anything extra-physical or spiritual in human personality? The experimental answer is, yes. There now is evidence that such an extra-physical factor exists in man. The soul hypothesis as defined has been established, but only as defined. Not the supernatural character of the soul, not its divine origin, its transmigration, its immortality—indeed nothing has been dealt with so far but its elemental reality."

The Rhines hold so important a position among contemporary psychical researchers that it will be useful to pause here and recount how they come to hold it. Professor Joseph Banks Rhine is the director of the Department of Parapsychology at Duke University, North Carolina. I met him during his European tour in 1950. He is a tall, shaggy, lumbering man, who impresses with his modesty, his friendly gentleness, and the air he has of a bashful missionary. He has a large, wise, kindly face, and broad, powerful shoulders. He was born shortly before the turn of the century at Rhine Hollow, Waterloo, Pennsylvania, a remote spot in the mountains, where the people commonly believed in omens, warnings, and messages from unseen agencies. His father, who was in turn a schoolmaster, a merchant, and a farmer, was completely sceptical concerning such things and taught the boy that these beliefs were mere superstitions.

While still a schoolboy Rhine became interested in religious and philosophical controversy. He argued interminably with the girl next door. This was Louisa Weckesser. She is now his wife, the mother of their four children, and his collaborator in much of his work.

Rhine served in the First World War with the U.S. Marines. He then enrolled as a student in Chicago University, where Miss Weckesser was already studying. They were married in April 1920, two years before they graduated. Both were botanists. They intended to make forestry their career. Then two things happened to change their lives. The first was a chance description of a psychic occurrence by a science teacher at Chicago University. The second was a lecture on Spiritualism delivered by Sir Arthur Conan Doyle.

"I went," says Rhine, "with many reservations, almost to scoff, and came away with the same reservations. But in spite of my doubts I carried away an impression that I still retain of what his belief had done to Sir Arthur. It had made him supremely happy."

These experiences, trivial though they may seem, led him to study psychology. He and his wife became students of Professor William McDougall, the British philosopher who was then teaching at Harvard, where the Rhines sought him out and entreated him to admit them to his courses. "I still regard McDougall as the greatest man I have ever met," Rhine says. When presently McDougall took up a post at Duke University the Rhines accompanied him, and together they founded the Department of Para-psychology, which is the name they gave to psychical research and cognate subjects. Since 1930 the Rhines have been initiating probes into Extra-sensory Perception, Precognition, Psychokinesis, Clairvoyance, and Telepathy. These subjects need to be defined.

Extra-sensory Perception (E.S.P. as it is called for short) is the power which some people possess of learning things without the use of any of the five senses. The Rhines and their staff at Duke investigated this power experimentally by means of Zener cards bearing five symbols, the Calculus of Probability and other mathematical and statistical aids. Mostly they persuaded their students in the department to name these cards before they were dealt. The conditions in which the calls were made were carefully devised to ensure that the subjects could not possibly know what cards were about to be turned up. Occasionally they called in outside helpers, such as professional mediums, clairvoyants, children, the mentally retarded, and the blind to check the results given by the others. There was also a series of experiments made with subjects at a considerable distance from the dealer of the Zener cards. By the laws of chance five correct hits might be expected out of a possible twenty-five, and five right was the average score of 80 per cent of the men and women tested, while others showed insignificant deviations. But one student, named Pearce, correctly called twenty-five cards in a row, another twenty-one, and several had seventeen and eighteen correct hits in a run through the Zener pack. The odds against Pearce's run of twenty-five correct calls being due to pure and undiluted chance were calculated to be 298,023,223,876,953,125 to 1. It was found too that the faculty of E.S.P. was diminished and even removed if the subject was given sodium amytal, a narcotic, but under a strong dose of caffeine it was restored. The best results were achieved when the subjects were stimulated to do their best by betting on the result. Usually the subjects had the best runs of correct calls at the beginning and end of the experiments, but their performances tended to slump during the middle of each session. Year after year, with incredible patience, the tests went on. Altogether upwards of a million calls were made forecasting the fall of the Zener cards by hundreds of subjects. All the results were noted and analysed. The result showed beyond reasonable doubt that some people do have knowledge conveyed to them by some means beyond the scope of the five senses; they could not merely be guessing right. At first it was argued by the critics of these experiments that the results were based on faulty mathematics, but this objection has now been abandoned. "If the Rhine investigation is to be fairly attacked," said Professor Camp, President of the Institute of Mathematical Statistics in 1937, "it must be on other than mathematical grounds."

It so happened, however, that when Dr. S. G. Soal, a mathematician at London University, tried to repeat Rhine's experiments in the late thirties he achieved only negative results. It was a full-scale test made with 120 people, who recorded 100,000 calls with the Zener cards in the psychology laboratory at University College, London. The subjects included Indians, Chinese, Egyptians, Greeks, Germans, Welsh, and other nationalities. Some were entranced mediums, and others were subjects in so deep a state of hypnosis that they felt no pain when sterilised hat-pins were stabbed into the backs of their arms. But no proof was given by any of these 120 persons that they were able either to "read thoughts" or "see without eyes" the figures on the Zener cards. What was at fault? Why did Rhine's experiment appear to succeed in America and Soal's fail in England? The answer was found after Dr. Soal had worked unsuccessfully for five years and recorded 128,350 calls that appeared to give no more than "chance" results according to the Calculus of Probability. Whately Carington then suggested to Dr. Soal that his subjects might be acting as Carington's had done in his own experiments in telepathy and in some manner "displacing" their calls: that is, correctly naming the card about to be turned up but either the next before or the next after it. Dr. Soal went through his records to see if this was so, and confirmed that this had indeed taken place in some instances. He thereupon revised his experiment in the light of this and satisfied both himself and his critics in the existence of Extra-sensory Perception.

Psychokinesis is the power of the mind to influence inanimate matter. To test whether this can in fact be done Professor Rhine experimented for nine years, throwing dice either by hand or by machines, and inciting his subjects to try and influence, by the power of their minds, what number would turn up. The results, again embracing thousands of instances, were all tabulated. Once more the mathematical results showed that some people do appear to have the ability of willing the behaviour of matter in certain instances.

The questions therefore arise: How can these faculties of Extra-sensory Perception and Psychokinesis be strengthened and used at will? The answers we do not yet know. All that seems to be certain at the moment is that E.S.P. and PK do exist in a weak and wayward state.

But Professor Rhine's work does not end with these researches. Another enquiry he has set on foot at Duke University is to find out whether animals have psychical powers similar to those of human beings. If it could be proved that they have, then a revolution would be effected in the attitude we commonly adopt when thinking about life itself, for it is customary to deny the possession of "souls" to non-humans. The Rhines have therefore seized upon the instances which from time to time are reported of the exceptional direction-finding ability of some animals. Is this ability psychic?

There is, for instance, the story of Bobbie, a collie, who was taken by motor-car from Oregon to Indiana. There Bobbie was lost after taking part in a dog-fight. Six months later he arrived home. His journey had taken him through cities, across rivers, deserts, and winter-locked mountains for 3,000 miles. He was so footsore and exhausted at the end of his journey that he lay for three days unable to walk. How did he find his way?

Another instance is that of Clementine, a large black cat, who was given to a neighbour when her mistress moved to a new home one thousand six hundred miles away. Yet Clementine traced her, though she had gone half-way across America. How?

Again, what is the explanation of the extraordinary feats of migration that birds achieve? The Pacific golden plover, for example, makes a 3,000-mile flight non-stop over the ocean from Alaska to the Hawaiian Islands with no landmarks to guide it, and other birds make every year no less bewildering journeys. Equally impressive is the single or group mind that flocks of wheeling starlings exhibit, and insects display a similar group mentality.

If animals do make use of what may be a psychic power, then it is more reliable, consistent, and widespread than any kindred faculty that has so far been discovered in humans. So at Duke University the Department of Para-psychology is assembling a collection of spontaneous instances of animal homing. These examples are not taken as evidence of psychic gifts, of course, but they may contribute the germ of an idea from which a workable hypothesis may later be worked out for experimental testing.

At home Rhine relaxes by tramping in the woods, swimming, and listening to music. But in the laboratory he is all energy in his quest for scientific facts. His mind is constantly reaching out for suggestions that will help him to explore that vague world he dimly perceives, a world that, fitfully and erratically, sends us occasionally a message without the help of our senses. That is for him the great mystery, the supreme challenge. "It is shocking but true," he has written, "that we know the atom today better than we know the mind that knows the atom." He has applied himself to repairing that strange gap in our knowledge.

During his tour of Europe in the summer of 1950 he lectured to the Royal Society of Medicine, the Society for Psychical Research, and the Universities of Oxford, Cambridge, Birmingham, and Manchester. He spoke on the Third Programme. He also lectured at continental universities and saw psychical experiments that are being conducted at Amiens, Innsbruck, Stockholm, Zürich, and Freiburg.

To the Royal Society of Medicine he said that laboratory experiments had established beyond reasonable doubt that such things as telepathy, clairvoyance, and E.S.P.—what are now being termed "psi phenomena"—are a fact. "Contrary to popular opinion," Professor Rhine said, "psi phenomena are not an abnormality; in fact in experiments in mental hospitals the results were no better than those with normal people; rather the reverse, because in my experience the people who are mentally well adjusted on the whole gave the best results. Dogs and other animals seem to possess marked telepathic powers, but this power tends to be deleted as the mind develops. In my opinion the psi phenomena are something on which psychiatrists may be able to provide a great deal of information." Accordingly he pleaded that this branch of the medical profession should co-operate in psychic research broadly defined. So many members came to hear him speak that an overflow meeting had to be held in another hall. It was the first time that the Royal Society of Medicine had been addressed on a subject of this sort.

To the Society for Psychical Research Professor Rhine said: "A case for survival has not been established to the satisfaction of any professional group, not even our own small group of para-psychologists, which is presumably the most favourably orientated one to be found. A hundred years of more or less scientific consideration of the survival question has left the scientific professions more unconvinced and more indifferent to the claims today than ever. During the last quarter of a century both public and professional interest in the problem has declined to a very marked extent."

There may, indeed, be diminished interest in this subject among professional scientists, but both in this country and in America the lay public is still avid for assurance that life, in some form, does continue after death. The increase in the number of adherents to the Spiritualistic doctrines and the amount of space given up by popular newspapers to the subject are indicative of this. Professor Rhine was on firmer ground when he went on to say that one reason for the failure of psychical research to make progress in its handling of the survival problem lies in the lack of methods for appraising impartially the statements made by mediums and in confusion over what the alternatives to the survival issue really are. "The great energies devoted to the investigation of the survival hypothesis were not turned," he pointed out, "as it now seems they should have been from the first, towards a thorough study of the powers attributable to the medium's own personality. Consequently there was no way of knowing what might have originated in the personalities of the discarnate so long as the range of the medium's own capacities was unknown. The worst disadvantage, however, from which the spirit hypothesis suffered in its investigation in the past was the fact that the issue was forced prematurely. The question whether the spirit survives bodily death depends first on whether there *is* anything like a spirit in man at all, or whether the belief that there is stands entirely without foundation in fact."

Professor Rhine insisted that those who have tackled the survival problem have tended to assume, more or less tacitly, not only that man has a spirit, but that when a person dies this spirit becomes endowed with powers it lacked on earth. Yet this assumption is pure speculation or is based on unverified mediumistic revelations. Neither convinced Spiritualists nor those who scoff at the notion of spirit survival find the present position agreeable: the latitude of doubt is too wide either way.

"If the lessons of the past mean anything," Professor Rhine argued, "the inquirer of the future will henceforth steer clear of entangling theologies and speculative hypotheses and plan a straightforward and thoroughgoing investigation of just what the distinction already found between the non-physical and the physical operations in personality means, and what more can be made of it in the understanding of the nature of the individual. With sufficient success in this exploration, the para-psychologist will find out what we all want to know— just how much of a differentiated mind or soul, or spirit, there is in man, and if there is any, what its powers and properties are. . . .

"The explorers in this beginning science are finally getting out of the blind alleys in which their predecessors have been wandering about much too fruitlessly during the last half century and more. Indeed, this escape from the intellectual traps in which so many inquirers have been caught might almost be hailed as a coming-of-age of this new branch of science. . . . The problems are urgent, the methods are ready, and not a few of the requisites of a science are at hand. Given time and a wise use of its opportunities, para-psychology will emerge as a full-bodied and effective science, playing a significant role on the stage of human thought. The outlook is not at all depressing."

This is the sternly scientific approach to a difficult problem. Nevertheless Rhine, in common with that other great psychical researcher, Whately Carington, has committed himself to the speculation that beyond the physical world we know there may be a non-physical world made up of bodiless minds in relation to each other. Carington wrote that he had, humanly speaking, no doubt at all that in some sense and in some degree man survives death, though he qualified this by saying that he was not at all sure about the sense and the degree of that survival, or about what survival means and how permanent it is.

Rhine has stated his hypothesis of a world of non-physical minds in his book, *The Reach of the Mind*. "The theory leads," he wrote, "to speculative views of a kind of psychical oversoul, or reservoir, or continuum, or universe, having its own system of laws and properties and potentialities. One can conceive of this great total pattern as having a transcendent uniqueness over and above the nature of its parts that some might call its divinity."

On this subject Professor Rhine's opinions seem to be crystallising, for in a recent number of the *Journal* which he publishes at Duke University he wrote: "Most people around the world today hold, and to some extent guide their lives by, a traditional belief that there is something in man that biologists do not know anything about.

"This belief is the one that holds to something indestructible, hence non-biological or immortal, in the human person. It would appear that only by the routes being opened up between para-psychology and biology can there be a successful investigation of the basis of this cultural belief by the methods and standards upon which biology itself has come to rely. Only thus can there be a closing of the gap, an integration of the knowledge with those treasured values by which most men have been guiding their lives.

"It is only by understanding life in all its major relationships that we can determine what we live by and what there is to live for, and do so with the larger degree of enlightenment that intelligent men everywhere demand."

Now that we have explored the historical setting of modern psychical research, its false starts, and its encumbrance of age-old prejudice, we can turn to the present practice of Spiritualism and go on to compare its tenets with those of orthodox Christianity.

CHAPTER IV

HOW SPIRITUALISM IS ORGANISED

SINCE everyone in Britain is free if he pleases to open a Psychic Centre or found a Spiritualist Church there is an ever-present danger that the opportunity thus afforded may be used for the practice of fraud or imposture. Because Spiritualists are jealous of their good name they have devised an elaborate organisation which embraces at a conservative estimate 1,000 churches and 50,000 adherents. Within this framework certain tests and sanctions are imposed, and if these are lightly and tolerantly applied they are, nevertheless, real and influential.

Four main groups of organised Spiritualists are to be discerned in this country. They are the Spiritualists' National Union, numerically the largest body; the Greater World Christian Spiritualist League; the White Eagle Lodges; and the Marylebone Spiritualist Association. In addition there are throughout Britain, especially in the larger towns, a considerable number of small, unorganised Spiritualist churches, but information about these is scanty and difficult to obtain. In this chapter these free-lances have had, willy-nilly, to be ignored, but it must be remembered that in the mass they must swell appreciably the numbers of those who accept the Spiritualist hypothesis of life after death with the possibility of communication between this world and the next.

In 1951 the Spiritualists' National Union had, according to its audited annual report, 491 churches with a total church membership of 19,003. Since 1944 the number of affiliated churches had increased by ninety-one and the church membership by almost 6,000. The S.N.U. was founded in 1890 by a number of leading Spiritualists in the North of England and its headquarters are still in Manchester. Nowadays, however, it is strongest in London, an area that for the Union's purposes spreads as far afield as Great Yarmouth. There are seventy-five affiliated churches with a membership of 4,278 in this district alone, compared with sixty-five (membership 1,795) in the North region. But this is only an ostensible superiority, because to the North's total must be added thirty-seven churches in Manchester, twenty-nine in North Lancashire, twenty-five in South-West Lancashire and Cheshire, twenty-five in Sheffield, and forty-two elsewhere in Yorkshire. Other districts embraced by the S.N.U. are the East and West Midlands, Scotland (with forty churches), the South, the South-West, and South Wales (which has thirty-nine churches).

Membership of the S.N.U. is open to individual Spiritualists and churches and kindred bodies. Its chief object is to promote the advancement and diffusion of the religion and religious philosophy of Spiritualism, the principles of which are explained in Chapter V. The Union aims at welding Spiritualist churches into a Spiritualist brotherhood and at securing for them full recognition as religious bodies. Further than this, it encourages Spiritualistic research; certifies lecturers, exponents, and teachers; publishes a substantial amount of Spiritualist literature; and promotes mission work. The Union helped to found the International Spiritualist Federation which unites Spiritualists in many countries, especially France, Holland, America, and Scandinavia.

Most Spiritualist churches do not have resident ministers or pastors, but are served by different exponents from week to week. Each church has full autonomy and may invite whom it likes. The Union has, however, compiled a register of recognised exponents of Spiritualism, and has further selected a number of these for appointment as National Spiritualist Ministers. These ministers do not take the title of "Reverend" or "Pastor"; in this they differ from the American practice. Of thirty-six accredited ministers in the London district, eleven are women. One of these ministers is Mr. Harry Edwards, a celebrated "psychic healer", and others are such noted mediums as Mrs. Bertha Harris, Miss Ursula Roberts, and Mr. Armand Wilson.

The work of the Spiritualists' National Union branches out in many directions. The Building of Churches, Education, Healing, Benevolence, Propaganda, and Defence are all vigorously conducted by democratically elected committees.

In the same year as the S.N.U. was founded the British Spiritualists' Lyceum Union came into being to care for the Spiritualist education of children and young people. The S.N.U. and the Lyceum Union amalgamated in 1948 and this "Sunday school" activity is now carried on as part of the regular work of the S.N.U. There are now 113 lyceums affiliated to the Union. Those churches which lack lyceums are constantly exhorted to "open the door for the children". Lyceums not only hold Sunday schools, but they also organise youth clubs and other activities for junior members of Spiritualist churches. Associate members are also enrolled. The chief purposes of the lyceums are to promote the study and practice of Spiritualism and to make suitable provision for training the young in social, physical, mental, moral, psychical, and spiritual matters. Many Spiritualist churches are licensed to conduct marriages. There is a recognised Spiritualist hymn-book. And a burial service has been devised to meet the special beliefs of Spiritualists.

Benevolence forms an important part of Spiritualist practice. In 1950 seventy pensioners were being supported by the S.N.U., involving an expenditure of £1,437. A Home of Rest scheme is also sponsored. In 1950, however, it was reported "with considerable concern" that 200 of the churches affiliated to the S.N.U. did not contribute to the Benevolence Fund. This does not imply, of course, that they did not carry on charities of their own.

The S.N.U is concerned to maintain a high standard of knowledge among those who expound Spiritualism, and accordingly it holds regular examinations which embrace such subjects as religion, philosophy, the history of Spiritualism, science, Spiritualistic phenomena, and mediumship. Of five who entered for one examination in mediumship two failed, and of the three who passed only one reached "credit" standard. Nine entered for a recent examination in Spiritualist teachings. Two did not sit, and of the remaining seven only one passed. Spiritualist healers are also closely watched, and a diploma examination has been arranged for them. One of the weaknesses shown by candidates, the S.N.U. asserts, is the lack of adequate and detailed records. They are reminded that records are essential and are of the utmost importance, it is said, for the protection of trance workers. Special Record Case Sheets have been drawn up.

Among the kindred bodies affiliated to the S.N.U. are the Bristol Society of Mediums, the Loughor Psychical Research Society, the Newcastle Psychical Research Institute, and the Portsmouth Mediums' Fellowship. Associated bodies include the British Mediums' Union, the Edinburgh Psychic College, and the Knight Crusaders.

The difference in doctrine between the Spiritualists' National Union and the Greater World Christian Spiritualist League will be explained in Chapter V. The League, the headquarters of which are in Holland Park, London, W.11, is considerably younger than the S.N.U., for it was not formed until May 1931. The churches affiliated to the G.W.C.S.L. at home and abroad number 388. They have a combined membership of 2,740 with 520 associates. Those who hold Greater World diplomas, certifying them as speakers and mediums, total 280. Membership of the League is international. There are members, diploma holders, and affiliated churches throughout the Commonwealth, the United States, and Europe, and in many places in the Near and Far East, including Burma and Japan. The League's journals are published in German, Dutch, and Danish, in addition to English. A Spanish number was published in 1934 and an Arabic number in 1935.

The League is interested in every aspect of Spirit Communion, but it neither practises nor encourages physical phenomena, such as apports, ectoplasmic materialisations, levitation, and so on. Instead, the League concentrates on teaching, psychic healing, and clairvoyance in the hope of bringing comfort, conviction, and help to others.

The business side of the League's work is handled by an Association Trust. This is a body with fifteen members forming a Committee of Management. In the basement of the League's headquarters is an extensive printing plant which is owned by the Association. On this machinery is produced the literature of the Association and the League, and much additional printing is done.

The League places strong emphasis on philanthropic work. In January 1933 Miss Winifred Moyes, the medium whose communications from a spirit control, known as Zodiac, led ultimately to the formation of the League, opened the first Greater World Free Night Shelter for homeless women at Lambeth. This shelter was destroyed by bombing in January 1945, after twelve years of activity on behalf of homeless women. Three years later the destroyed shelter was replaced by a new one at Deptford. Meanwhile an extensive shelter had been opened at Leeds in 1935. The Leeds shelter has dormitories for thirty women. Breakfast, supper, bed, and renewal of clothing are provided free of charge. The London shelter is said to be used each year by nearly 19,000 women who would otherwise be sleeping out-of-doors. They are fed night and morning without charge. Hundreds have been entirely reclothed and many have been found work. The running of both shelters is undertaken by a large staff of volunteers. At Leigh-on-Sea a convalescent home is carried on. And in Kennington and Leyton there are depots for helping distressed cases.

Normally the League accepts no church for affiliation until it has been in continuous active existence for at least six months. No fees or subscriptions are compulsorily levied, either for affiliation or for granting diplomas or certificates. The League's work is carried on entirely by means of free-will offerings and as far as possible by voluntary service. The League does not interfere with the internal management of churches so long as their constitutions are satisfactory. It is, however, always glad to help and advise should difficulties be met. The League urges that all churches affiliated to it should, for propaganda purposes, include the word "Christian" in their title. When new churches are inaugurated it is asked that they should be sufficiently far away from existing churches to avoid drawing away any part of their congregations. Great importance is placed by the League on Bible study. The Authorised Version is the standard Bible of the League, and all affiliated churches are asked to adopt it for general use. All churches are exhorted to form Bible Study Classes, enlisting the help of all who are qualified to teach.

In common with, I believe, all Spiritualist churches, the League attaches great importance to the work of psychic healing. It organises a Fellowship of Prayer for undertaking "absent healing". The League's periodical, *The Greater World*, publishes a form in each number which readers may use to obtain "absent healing" for the sick. They write in the name of the person for whom prayer is desired and state the complaint of the sufferer. They add their own name and address. The form includes a "monthly report" under the three headings: "quite well", "condition improving", and "no change". The reader is asked to strike out the lines not applicable when returning the form to the Fellowship. A week's work at the League's Sanctuary in Holland Park includes a Saturday evening service, healing service and treatment on Tuesday afternoon, addresses and clairvoyance on Wednesday afternoon and evening, a healing service and treatment on Thursday evening, and on Sunday an Intercession service followed by treatment in the morning, a Children's Sunday School in the afternoon, and an evening service including an address and clairvoyance. A French service is held on the last Saturday in each month at 3 p.m. and a German service on the first Wednesday in each month at 7 p.m.

This pattern of activity is followed closely by churches affiliated to the League. At the Sanctuary of the Spirit,

Morden, for example, there is usually a Sunday-evening
service with an address and clairvoyance, an absent healing
service on Monday night, and healing services on Tuesday,
Wednesday, and Thursday. All healing servies at this church
are conducted under trance by Dr. Grant and his band of
spirit doctors through the mediumship of Mrs. D. M. James.
Many of the League's churches hold Holy Communion services once a month. Catford Christian Spiritualist Church is
one of these, and among its other activities are trance healing by White Eagle through the mediumship of Mrs. Emily
Johnson on Monday evening, a Transfiguration Service on
Wednesday night, demonstrations of psychometry on Thursday and Saturday afternoons and evenings, and absent heal-
ing and sittings by appointment. Leeds, Sheffield, Cleethorpes,
Northampton, and elsewhere throughout the country have
League Churches doing similar work. Bristol has a Christian
Spiritualist Temple which adds a Nursing and Residential
Home to its activities.

On a far smaller scale than either the Spiritualists' National
Union or the Greater World Christian Spiritualist League are
the White Eagle Lodges. The mother lodge is located at St.
Mary Abbot's Place, Kensington, London, W.8, and there
are daughter lodges in Scotland and America. The London
Lodge, which was founded in 1936, has about 400 members.
Its leader is Mrs. Grace Cooke. The White Eagle Lodge
is registered at Somerset House as an undenominational
Christian Church. Spiritual healing is an important activity.
The London Lodge treats about 400 patients every week.
A large proportion of these are said to be sufferers for whom
medicine can do little more. Most of them have been recommended to seek spiritual healing from the White Eagle Lodge
by former patients who have received help in this way. This
sanctuary has already more patients than it can comfortably
handle. The Lodge believes that its most important activity
is to disseminate the teaching and philosophy of White Eagle,
its spirit guide. It publishes a number of books embodying
his precepts, and, every other month, a journal, *Stella Polaris*.

The Marylebone Spiritualist Association, which occupies extensive premises in Russell Square, London, W.C.1, is thought to be the largest Spiritualist association in the world. Founded in 1872, its membership now exceeds 7,000, and though from time to time it has moved its headquarters to different parts of London it continues to keep the name of its original home in its title. The Association lacks a church of its own, and holds its Sunday evening services in the basement of a large block of offices in Bloomsbury Square. The purpose of the M.S.A. is to provide an organisation through which survival after death may be investigated, communication with the spirit world established, psychic phenomena studied, and the desire for spiritual development and the search for truth promoted in many directions, all under satisfactory conditions and with proper safeguards. It also forms a centre where workers from the spirit world may bring proofs of survival, comfort, healing, and instructions to its members and help them to realise their essential unity with the world of spirit. The Association is not antagonistic to any religious belief. Membership is, therefore, entirely non-sectarian and open to everyone—of any belief or none.

The M.S.A. has weathered many vicissitudes. At the end of its first eight years it had only thirty members. It has lost its premises again and again. Once it was evicted by a critical clergyman. Its services each Sunday in the Queen's Hall ended, with so much else, when that beloved building was destroyed by bombing in the last war. And it occupies its present headquarters on a yearly basis only by agreement with the Ministry of Works. Despite all these difficulties it is now one of the foremost Spiritualist organisations in the country.

The activities of the M.S.A. include religious services every Sunday, lectures on all aspects of Spiritualism and kindred subjects, classes for the study of Higher Teaching and psychic development, discussion and research groups, spiritual and mental healing, the testing of mediums, group seances, arranging private sittings with mediums, and demonstrations of

c

clairvoyance, clairaudience, psychometry, and physical phenomena. It has gathered together a library of 5,000 books on
psychic subjects. Every year it organises on Armistice Sunday
a Service of Reunion in the Royal Albert Hall, London, when
upwards of 5,000 people attend. At these Reunion Services
musicians of the calibre of Isobel Baillie and Hervey Allan
are engaged to sing, leading mediums demonstrate, and distinguished Spiritualists testify to their faith.

On most weekdays the headquarters of the M.S.A. from
1 p.m. until late in the evening are bustling with activity.
Psychic healing is, naturally, an important aspect of the work,
and is led by a well-known Spiritualist healer and medium,
Mrs. Nan Mackenzie, whose name is honoured throughout
the movement. She is, however, only one of the many psychic
healers taking part in this work. Elsewhere in the building
groups are meeting to develop their psychic gifts, mediums
are being consulted by members, psychometry and clairvoyance are being demonstrated, and lectures on Spiritualist
topics are being delivered. Typewriters *clack* away in the
ground floor office, where appointments are arranged for
members, books issued from the library, and literature is
sold. Even a casual visit to the building is enough to show
how intense and widespread is the present interest in Spiritualist matters. The impression that the layman takes away is
that with the M.S.A. the emphasis tends to fall on the practical
rather than on the religious aspect of Spiritualism, though
the religious aspect is by no means negligible.

In all organised Spiritualism there is lively concern regarding the integrity of mediums. For this reason most Spiritualist
bodies tend, in their public work at least, to disregard the
work of those who are known as "physical mediums". These
are the men and women who assert they can produce materialisations either in the form of apports, ectoplasm (the substance of the spirit "body"), talking trumpets that float at
will, or furniture that moves without the aid of any discernible
force. Physical mediumship is especially subject to criticism
because of the darkness in which it is invariably demonstrated.

Moreover, it is commonly declared that to interfere with a medium during one of these "physical" demonstrations may result in serious injury to him and even his death. It is therefore peculiarly difficult to arrange these demonstrations under test conditions, such as a scientist in a laboratory would most certainly insist upon. Because of the manner in which physical mediums work, they have, it is known, been tempted frequently to practise fraud. Ectoplasm can be simulated by cheesecloth. Modern conjuring can stage tricks that perfectly counterfeit many alleged apports. All this has combined to discredit a great deal of physical mediumship, and so Spiritualist organisations have grown shy of sponsoring it in public. This does not mean that all physical mediumship is nowadays suspected *a priori* of being fraudulent by discerning Spiritualists. On the contrary, many of them attach great importance to materialisations and hold many physical mediums in high respect. But despite this it is believed to be better to rely, for demonstrations in churches and public halls, on "mental" mediumship such as clairvoyance, clairaudience, and psychometry (the divining of the past by handling various objects).

Two of my colleagues, men of exceptional distinction, while investigating psychic phenomena a quarter of a century ago, had an opportunity to sit with an apport medium in London. Before the sitting, they told me, they minutely searched the seance room for half an hour. They found nothing suspicious. They then examined the medium without finding anything concealed in his clothes. The room was then blacked out except for a dim red light. By the aid of this they saw floating megaphones from which voices were heard and similar phenomena. At the end of the sitting the medium began to tug and strain at something on the floor. The light was then switched on and the medium handed to my colleagues a clump of lilies-of-the-valley with moist soil still about the roots. They divided the clump between them, took their portions home, and planted them in their gardens where they struck root. A conjuring trick? If it was, then, say my friends, they are completely baffled to explain it after the precautions they took.

One of the best known of apport mediums was Charles Bailey, of Sydney, Australia. Accounts have been published of how Bailey would strip, encase his hands in boxing-gloves, and have himself covered in a kind of sleeping bag from head to foot. In the rooms where he held his seances there was reported to be no other furniture than a row of kitchen chairs for the comfort of his sitters, who were directed to search each other before the seance began. Under these stringent conditions, Bailey is said to have materialised live birds from India, Malaya, and elsewhere, birds'-nests with either eggs or unfledged chicks from Egypt and India; live fish from the South Pacific, a six-foot-long leopard's skin, and ancient Egyptian papyri. Also among his apports were one hundred ancient coins, exotic shrubs, precious stones, a skull, and a portion of Indian tapestry that was found to measure 11 feet by 5 feet. Mr. Stanley Breck, writing in the American psychic magazine, *Chimes,* for March 1952, tells how he attended a seance with Bailey in 1940. The medium was at that time an extremely old man. Nevertheless he was still producing apports, and after the seance Mr. Breck says that he carefully packed up a number of specimens and took them back with him to America. Among these were clay tablets covered with writing in cuneiform characters. Mr. Breck later sent these tablets to Lord Dowding in London and suggested that it would be interesting if the writing could be translated at the British Museum. Mr. Breck received this reply from Lord Dowding: "I took the apports to the British Museum and you will be sorry to hear that the clay tablets were pronounced without hesitation to be fakes. The man quite obviously knew what he was talking about. He had lived for some time in Iraq and he was fairly sure that he knew the village where they had been forged and the man who had forged them. This man made a handsome income by selling forged tablets to the troops. Of course, the fact that the tablets are fakes does not necessarily bar their having been apports." This experience shows the difficulty of forming an objective opinion concerning physical mediumship. And even if certain apports are accepted as indubitably genuine what exactly does it "prove" to have a flying fish from the South Seas materialise in a seance room or an Egyptian papyrus come fluttering to the floor? There is no one answer to that question. . . .

All certificated mediums are repeatedly directed by their sponsors to practise arduously to develop their psychic gifts, at the same time guarding against the danger of exhausting these by overworking them. The London Spiritualist Alliance publishes a manual by Helen Macgregor and Margaret V. Underhill which instructs would-be mediums how to develop their psychic faculties. The medium has to be both physic-ally fit and mentally adjusted. Sunshine and fresh air are to be sought, but because many psychics are extremely sensitive to direct sunlight on the head they are advised to wear hats when taking sun-baths. The medium has also to study the vitamin content of his diet and ensure that vitamins and mineral salts are not wasted by overcooking. Many mediums are vegetarians, but vegetarianism is not obligatory, for some psychics find it better to eat meat in moderation. They are advised not to eat a large meal before a sitting, and a number of mediums prefer to come fasting to a seance. Mediums have to acquire the art of controlled relaxation so as not to interfere with the flow of nerve energy. It is important not to concentrate on mediumship to the exclusion of all other interests. Those who make mediumship their profession are advised to take up a secondary art or study, especially one which will require them to use their minds and bodies skil-fully. It is stressed that no genuine medium can expect to be 100 per cent successful; all will experience failure from time to time. Macgregor and Underhill suggest such exercises for mediums as imagining themselves surrounded by a particular colour for as long as they desire—a difficult feat; practising visualisation by looking at objects and memorising their characteristics—shape, size, colour, and so on; and covering the eyes with the hands to exclude all light and then trying to see black and only black even after the hands have been removed.

The material rewards to which the practising medium can look forward are not large. An average fee for a sitting is, I am told, half a guinea. Even for a demonstration in a church before, perhaps, 400 or 500 people, the fee paid is usually about one guinea to a visiting medium, with, of course, expenses. Sittings with groups are naturally more profitable, because then the members of the circle will each pay perhaps five shillings or seven-and-sixpence and the total thus raised may amount to thirty shillings or £2. I am told that the income of an average medium probably varies between £7 and £9 a week, which is not a large reward for so precarious and wearing a profession. A medium possessed of unusual gifts, however, may become fashionable and arouse widespread eagerness among the wealthy to sit with him. One of these, and they are not numerous, may charge up to three guineas for a single sitting and still be able to turn away clients clamouring for his services. But no one undertaking mediumship can expect a lucrative income over many years. The work is essentially a vocation.

America may possibly afford richer rewards. California especially has embraced Spiritualism and has at least eighty-seven Spiritualist churches, of which twenty-nine are in Los Angeles and six in Hollywood. Chicago has at least fifteen of these churches and New York twelve. They go by such names as The Temple of Eternal Life and Light, The Psychic Science Temple of Divine Brotherhood, and the La Verne Temple of Brotherhood Illumination. Long Beach, California, has its Temple in the Sky, the terrestrial address of which is the Villa Riviera Hotel, suite 1508. It is the custom in America for the Spiritualist churches to be led by a minister or pastor who commonly takes the title of "Reverend". The activities of the American Spiritualist churches are similar to those of Britain. At San Francisco, for example, the Spiritualist Church of Revelation holds services every Thursday at 7.45 p.m. when materialisation and direct voice medium-ship is demonstrated; and in the same city the Little Church of Spiritualism holds Sunday services, healing demonstrations on Thursday evenings, and "unfoldment" classes on Tuesdays and Wednesdays. In Chicago the Friendly Spiritualist Church, in addition to services every Sunday night, holds a Sacred Candle service on the first Sunday in every month. The weekly programme of New York's United Spiritualists' Church covers healing and a lecture on Sunday and Tuesday, messages on Wednesday and Friday, and a Bible Study class on Monday. Generally it is messages from the spirit world, psychic heal-ing, and Sunday-school work on which the American churches concentrate, as do those of Britain.

It is not my intention to offer any criticism of the American approach to Spiritualism, but it does differ from the European. The American idiom and outlook is often sharply opposed to ours, and it is always necessary to remember this when comparing America and Britain. I doubt if in this country any "certified medium and healer" would confidently advertise "my guide can answer your most important question. Enclose one dollar and postage", or "I guarantee to answer 6 of 8 questions. Send date of birth, self-addressed envelope, and two dollars". Most responsible British Spiritualists would be sceptical of such offers. Their experience does not accord with such methods, and it is a commonplace for them to insist that no medium can obtain results for every sitter. But adver-tisements such as those I have quoted are common in the psychic press of America. Mostly the mediums who advertise in this way ask those who respond to send a "love offering". Nor is there any shyness across the Atlantic about advertising correspondence courses in Spiritual Development. Sound films are also used to promote the missionary work of Spiritualism. All this Americans unhesitatingly accept as normal, legitimate activity.

The American attitude is crystallised in this advertisement of California's Chapel in the Sky, which is accompanied by a photograph of the Rev. C. Richard Minugh, metaphysician:

"Every morning Dr. Richard Minugh sends a Divine Healing Prayer Vibration to his students and all who seek his help in healing and liberating themselves from physical or mental disease or the spiritual suffering of ignorance. Anyone who wishes to avail himself of this help, which Dr. Minugh is happy to extend to all, may write to the Chapel in the Sky, briefly stating the nature of his or her trouble. There is no charge except what is given as a freewill offering to help spread this Spiritual Healing work." There speaks America. Spiritualism, as we have seen, was brought to this country from America one hundred years ago. Whether the future of the movement will be along the lines of the present British conception or the American is an interesting speculation.

CHAPTER V

HEAVEN AND HELL

Most forms of Spiritualism differ from orthodox Christianity over the doctrine of the divinity of Christ. The majority of Spiritualists do not accept Jesus as Saviour. They regard Him as the perfect exemplar in whose person is personified the Life Ideal. There is, however, as we shall see, a powerful minority who do accept Christ as the Son of God. This sharp clash of doctrine on a crucial point of theology makes it difficult to generalise about Spiritualism as a religion. I imagine that it is the rejection, by the majority party, of belief in the divinity of Christ that has aroused much of the distress, and even enmity, of churchgoers when contemplating Spiritualism. And yet the Spiritualists' attitude is not lightly assumed. It springs from one of their fundamental principles—that all men on earth are responsible for their own actions and must account for them, not at the Day of Judgment, but so soon as they pass over to the other side. The spirits, it is held, can teach, uplift, and inspire the living on the earthly plane, but they are powerless to affect human actions. The only exception to this doctrine, it seems, comes from certain evil spirits who, being unable to shake off their ties with earth, take possession of human minds and lead their hosts into wrong-doing, madness, or even self-destruction. This principle of personal responsibility is the fifth of seven fundamental tenets recognised by members of the Spiritualists' National Union which, as we saw in the last chapter, represents the majority of those belonging to the movement. The other six basic principles are:

The Fatherhood of God.
The Brotherhood of Man.

73

The Communion of Saints and the Ministry of Angels.

The continuous existence of the human soul.

Compensation and retribution hereafter for all the good and evil deeds done on earth.

Eternal progress open to every human soul.

Although these principles are regarded as basic by the Spiritualists' National Union, liberty of interpretation is assured to each member.

The Greater World Christian Spiritualist League, the next largest organisation within the movement, believe in a different theology from that taught by the Spiritualists' National Union. They accept the leadership of Jesus Christ and explicitly believe in His divinity in its full sense, that He was born of the Virgin Mary and was the promised Messiah.

The League's creed is repeated in its 388 churches at their Sunday services. The other clauses are:

I believe in one God who is love.

I believe that God manifests through the illimitable power of the Holy Spirit.

I believe in the survival of the human soul and its individuality after physical death.

I believe in the communion with God, with his angelic ministers, and with the souls functioning in conditions other than the earth life.

I believe that all forms of life created by God intermingle, are interdependent, and evolve until perfection is attained.

I believe in the perfect justice of the divine laws governing all life.

I believe that sins committed can only be rectified by the sinner himself, through the redemptive power of Jesus Christ, by repentance and service to others.

Members of the League take this pledge: "I will at all times endeavour to be guided in my thoughts, words and deeds by the teaching and example of Jesus Christ."

The League's doctrine is based on the teachings of Zodiac, who is the spirit control of Miss Winifred Moyes, through whose mediumship he first communicated in 1921 at a private circle of three sitters. Miss Moyes is nowadays an honorary vice-president of the League and, until her severe illness at Christmas 1950, one of its most active workers. From the first, Zodiac's addresses aroused widespread interest among Spiritualists, for they were freely circulated after being recorded in shorthand. In August 1928 Zodiac gave his first public address, and these addresses continued to be given weekly, in public halls and Spiritualist churches, almost without a break, until Miss Moyes's illness. Since then he has communicated on only two occasions. The League hopes there will be a recovery later and that Zodiac will resume his addresses. Meanwhile, representatives from the League's headquarters in Lansdown Road, Holland Park, London, W.11, take services as required at churches affiliated to the League.

Members of the Greater World Christian Spiritualist League attach signal importance to the communications of Zodiac because they believe he is the spirit of the scribe, mentioned in the twelfth chapter of St. Mark, who asked Jesus which is the first commandment of all. And when he was told it was monotheism and the love of one's neighbours, he replied: "Well, Master, thou hast said the truth: for there is one God; and there is none other but he: and to love him with all the heart and with all the understanding, and with all the soul, and with all the strength, and to love his neighbour as himself, is more than all burnt offerings and sacrifices. And when Jesus saw that he answered discreetly," St. Mark adds, "he said unto him, Thou art not far from the kingdom of God."

It is noteworthy that Zodiac is one of the rare instances in which the spirit of someone mentioned in the Bible is supposed to have communicated through a medium. It is this which heightens in the eyes of many Spiritualists the theological importance of Zodiac's teaching, and explains how the League's doctrines come to be framed on what are largely orthodox Christian lines.

The beliefs of the White Eagle Lodges, whose leader is Mrs. Grace Cooke, branch out in a different direction. Members reject the name "church" for the places in which their services are held. They prefer to call them "Lodges", which they define as places where people assemble to rest and find refreshment, mingling in true spiritual comradeship. A Lodge, they say, is the recognised home of a brotherhood—a word which signifies a group of people kept together with a family spirit, alive and active in its Father's business. To their way of thinking a church implies a building used chiefly on Sundays and standing empty and idle for most of the rest of the week.

White Eagle is the spirit guide of these people, and he is the messenger through whom has come the teaching and philosophy animating the Lodges. White Eagle comes from a spiritual brotherhood in the other world known as the White Brotherhood. The members believe that as times change so spiritual truth has periodically to be restated in accordance with changed conditions. They hold that spiritual truth today has to be restated so that it is freed from dogma or creed and is gentle, simple, and tolerant of all other men's beliefs.

Members of White Eagle Lodges are not primarily concerned, as so many other Spiritualists are, to prove survival. They themselves sometimes question whether theirs can be called a Spiritualist church in the accepted sense. Certainly the parent Lodge, at St. Mary Abbots Place, Kensington, London, W.8, is registered at Somerset House as an "undenominational" Christian church. The one ritualistic aspect of their services is that the officiating minister wears a robe or surplice.

The teachings of the White Eagle Lodges are:

The Father-Motherhood of God.
That Christ, the Son of the Father-Mother God, is the light which shines through the Wisdom and Love in the human heart; and that by reason of this Divine Sonship all are brothers and sisters regardless of race, class, or creed; and that this brotherhood and sisterhood embraces life visible and invisible.

The expression of these principles in daily life through service.

The awareness of the invisible world which bridges separation and death, and reveals the eternal unity of life.

That life is governed by five cosmic laws: Reincarnation; Cause and Effect; Opportunity; Correspondences (as above, so below); Equilibrium (the Law of Compensation).

The ultimate goal of mankind is the blooming of the Rose at the Heart of the Cross; the realisation of the Christ-Consciousness as exemplified by the Master; the reunion of the Holy Family.

The symbol of the White Eagle Lodges is a cross within a circle with a six-pointed star at its heart. Members show a lively interest in astrology.

The philosophy taught in these Lodges is based upon the conception of man as primarily a spiritual being. Understanding, it is taught, is to be found by a process of spiritual unfolding within each person. This is not an intellectual development, but the nurturing of the spirit long hungry and neglected in man. Fostered in this way, understanding can explain the purpose of human suffering and how it is to be relieved, and can provide peace at heart and a resultant steadfast happiness based upon an inner quietude. From this spring, again, health of body, harmony of mind, and upliftment of soul.

White Eagle's teaching is thus epitomised: "God has destined man to be happy. Only because men stray far from God do they become frightened, lonely, lost." He proclaims a religion of happiness open to every man, woman, and child, and asserts that happiness shall be the religion of the New Age. This happiness will be enjoyed and retained only so long as it is shared with others.

The Lodges strive to embody this teaching in the work they do. They are at considerable pains to make their sanctuaries beautiful and tranquil. Here the members worship every Sunday. Regular lectures are given. Study and meditation groups meet. The sanctuaries are open five days every week, and the workers in them are ready to receive anyone requiring help in dealing with their particular problems in the light of the spiritual laws governing life. The members are especially concerned to comfort and encourage the bereaved. White Eagle's teaching, it is said, has renewed many a human life and healed many a saddened heart.

Spiritual healing—a subject that will be studied at length later in this book—forms an important part of Lodge work. Two forms are practised—absent healing and contact healing. Absent healing is for those who cannot attend in person, and many sufferers are treated by this method. Trained healers are available for contact healing, and for this work small and beautiful chapels are set apart. About 400 patients are treated every week. A large proportion of them are stricken people for whom conventional medicine holds out no hope. All Lodge members are asked to help, if possible, with this work of healing, but it is emphasised that the London Lodge has already more patients than it can comfortably deal with.

White Eagle's followers concentrate mainly on the philosophy of life unfolded by the world beyond. The Lodges provide for those members, together with others of many other sects, who have been convinced of survival by Spiritualism and who are asking what follows after. It has thus come to be regarded as the most important of the activities of the London Lodge that it should produce and distribute books containing the doctrines and philosophy of White Eagle. These books are now being read in a large number of countries.

Once inquirers have been convinced to their own satisfaction that the dead survive, the next question they commonly ask is, what is the nature of the Spirit World? What is the truth about life in heaven and in hell? Because of the divergence of Spiritualist teaching, the answers given by the different sects are sometimes at variance, just as their theology does not always agree. What follows, therefore, is an outline of some of the best-known Spiritualist books that have met with wide acceptance within the movement.

The most important of these books is Stainton Moses's *Spirit Teachings*, first published about 1883. Stainton Moses was the son of the headmaster of a Lincolnshire grammar school. He graduated at Oxford, took Holy Orders, and at the age of twenty-four became a curate in the Isle of Man. The work he did during an epidemic of smallpox brought him into prominence. He held other ecclesiastical appointments, but ill-health forced him to give up his church career and he took work as a private tutor and schoolmaster. He was moved to embark upon an investigation of Spiritualism, thinking to expose it as fraudulent, but within six months he had become convinced of its essential truth. Soon he was one of the great figures of the Spiritualist movement. He was found to be a notable medium, particularly in that branch of mediumship known as automatic writing, when spirit agents are supposed to use the medium's hand involuntarily to take down messages. It was in this manner that *Spirit Teachings* was composed, the control for the most part being a spirit known as Impera-tor. Ever since its first publication *Spirit Teachings* has been one of the classics of Spiritualism. The first message was con-veyed by Stainton Moses's hand on March 30, 1873, about one year after his introduction to Spiritualism, and messages continued to be received until 1880. What is important to note about Stainton Moses's mediumship is his cultural back-ground and theological training. Here it is legitimate to add, I think, that Renan's *Life of Christ* had been published ten years previously and formed part of the intellectual climate of his time. I hazard the guess that Renan's interpretation of Christianity may have powerfully influenced Stainton Moses's religious thinking, though in his opinion Imperator's messages came to him from a source outside himself and this opinion is generally accepted by Spiritualists.

Moses had been trained, as he himself insists, in strict accordance with Protestant Church principles. He had read extensively the theologies of the Greek and Roman Churches, and he had accepted, as most nearly according with the views at which he had arrived, the tenets of the Church of England.

Before he became a practising Spiritualist he had revised some of his more extreme beliefs, but substantially he was what most people would have termed a sound High Churchman. In this he is unique among mediums. As a Spiritualist medium is but a channel of communication, constraining and to some extent moulding the character of the messages he receives, so the movement points out, his background may help partly to explain the character of Imperator's teaching.

This spirit guide, we soon recognise, was more concerned to instil in Stainton Moses a reformed religion for modern needs than to enlighten him concerning the details of life in the world of spirit. At the very beginning of his communications he emphasises that now, as ever in the history of the world, there is a conflict between good and evil. The efforts of the messengers of God are resisted by what he calls the hosts of the adversaries. God's messengers are spirit guides whose natural aptitude is to teach. They are drawn from the three lower spheres or states of being in the spirit world. They are opposed by adversaries who strive to frustrate the work of the messengers by counterfeiting their influence and by inciting other men and spirits to combat the powers of goodness. Adversaries are spirits who have chosen evil. They are led by Intelligences still more evil to malign the messengers and hamper their work. Their activity manifests itself in evil passions and in presenting to inquiring souls that which is mean and base where the messengers would tenderly lead to the noble and pure. The adversaries are the foes of God and man. They are enemies of goodness, the ministers of evil. Against them the messengers wage perpetual war. These adversaries are the spirits of those who have yielded to the lusts of a sensual body which finally became their slave. They are recruited from the masses of unprogressed, undeveloped spirits who have turned against penitance and refused the gradual and laborious undoing of sin and sinful habit. They are governed by many chiefs, but Imperator expressly repudiates the existence of the Satan of the theologians. Spirits, good and bad alike, he taught, are subject to the rule of commanding intelligences.

The adversaries are specially attracted by all that is debased on earth. They are, in fact, earth-bound. The "Hell" they inhabit is none other than this earth. They retain much of their earthly passion and propensity. Their sensual cravings are not extinct, though they have lost the means of gratifying them. The drunkard's old thirst is intensified by the impossibility of slaking it. Unquenched, it urges him back to his old haunts, where he drives men to further degradation. Within the earthly drunkard he relives his old life and derives a grim and devilish satisfaction from the orgies he incites him to embark upon. On such an occasion as Derby Day, Imperator declared, the adversaries mass together in great force, to attack those fevered with the hope of coming gains or plunged into despair because they have lost everything. Imperator abhorred race-meetings and all such gatherings.

The religion he expounded was the three-fold one of duty to God, duty to man, and duty to self. Worship fulfils the duty to God. The duty to man is met by helping one's neighbours onward in the path of progress. Duty to self embraces an elaborate code. The physical body is to be tended and guarded. Every means must be cultivated of extending knowledge. Spiritual growth must be earnestly sought. There must be no staining of a man's integrity, and he must hold firmly in all things to what he knows to be right and good. Finally communion with the world of spirit must be cultivated by prayer and frequent intercourse.

From all this it follows that our experience of earth-life is essential and cannot be dispensed with. Those who die in infancy cannot, therefore, pass immediately to one of the higher spheres, but must first remedy their lack of experience and knowledge by training and education at the hands of spirits charged with their instruction and supplying them with what they have missed.

It was Imperator who taught that Christ was neither divine nor the Saviour. "We know that no spirit more pure, more godlike, more noble, more blessing and more blessed ever descended to find a home on your earth," he wrote through the hand of Stainton Moses. "None more worthily earned by a life of self-sacrificing love the adoring reverence and devotion of mankind. None bestowed more blessings on humanity; none wrought a greater work for God. . . . We do not dishonour the Lord Jesus—before whose exalted majesty we bow—by refusing to acquiesce in a fiction which He would disown, and which man has forced upon His name. . . . The attributing to a man of divine honour, to the exclusion in very many cases of personal honour and love for the Great Father, is a mischievous error which derogates from the duty of man to his God. . . . 'The letter,' says your Scripture, 'the letter killeth, but the spirit giveth life.' Hence we denounce such views of God as are contained in the fable of a material hell; and we proclaim to you purer and more rational ideas than are contained in the orthodox notions of atonement and vicarious sacrifice. We proclaim to you a spiritualised religion." Imperator went on to say, a little later, that the keynote of the religion he was teaching was the immortality of man, held not as an article of faith, a clause in a creed, but as a piece of personal knowledge and individual experience.

One more point in Imperator's teaching must be mentioned here because of its bearing on Chapter VIII of this book, in which I shall describe the Spiritualist's attitude towards demoniac possession. Imperator expressly forbids anyone of unbalanced mind to meddle with the mysteries of mediumship. It is a dire risk to them. He deprecates always any unlicensed meddling. Only those who are guarded by the messengers, only those who act from no inner motive but in obedience to the impulse of the controlling guardians, who are wise and powerful to protect, should act as mediums and then only carefully and with earnest prayer. He insists that mediums must be of even mind and steady temper. Anyone of unhinged mind, spasmodic temperament, and fitful purposeless character becomes the ready prey of undeveloped, evil, earth-bound spirits. It is an injunction and a warning that responsible Spiritualists have never forgotten.

About half a century after Stainton Moses wrote his famous

book, the Rev. C. Drayton Thomas published *Life Beyond Death,* which is detailed on the very points where Imperator inclines to be vague, most concrete where he is apt to fade into shadowiness. Drayton Thomas, like his father before him, was a Methodist minister. It is from his father and his sister, Etta, that the messages he relates in his book emanate. Unlike Stainton Moses, Drayton Thomas was not his own medium. Instead, he sat with Mrs. Osborne Leonard, one of the most reputable mediums this country has ever produced. She acted for Sir Oliver Lodge, and sat innumerable times for the Society for Psychical Research. Drayton Thomas was not a passive sitter. On the contrary. Like the Queen of Sheba in the presence of King Solomon, he tried his father and his sister, through the medium, with many hard questions, and it is from the lengthy answers he received over many years that a detailed picture can be drawn of life in heaven and in hell as the Spiritualist believes it to be.

First of all, the notion of angelic choirs playing harps through all eternity is dispelled, and so is that of an ever-lasting fiery pit in which the souls of the damned are burned. As with Stainton Moses we hear of "spheres" or states of being on the other side through which the spirit ever progresses. These spheres surround the earth in space and form a series of globes. The highest sphere is the ultimate heaven. The lowest sphere of all is the habitation of the evil. In the sphere immediately above the lowest are the spirits of the weak and selfish who on earth sinned by omitting to do right rather than by deliberately injuring their fellows. Immediately the dead pass over they enter their appropriate sphere. Drayton Thomas's father and his sister, for example, entered the third sphere, and it is here where most of the dead begin their training. In the other world, the dead take on their spiritual or etheric body. This etheric body is at first conditioned by what was done in the flesh, so that on first passing over the punishment for shortcomings and wrong-doing on earth is a limited and handicapped etheric body. Nevertheless the dead, at least those in the third sphere, resemble in their etheric body what they had looked like on earth when at the peak of their physical and spiritual powers. They even choose, as a rule, to dress much as they did while on earth, creating their clothes by a process of thought. In this wise they remain until they are eventually joined by those they have loved on earth and for whom they are waiting. When the reunion is complete all begin slowly to change. This transformation normally takes place in groups of spirits, who are able to mould their appearance to their will far more than is possible when in the flesh. They need neither food nor drink, for they breathe in their nourishment. They never feel tired. They do not sleep, and never lose consciousness, though from time to time they rest. Long walks and gardening are favourite relaxations, just as architecture and building are activities in which many spirits find keenest pleasure. Spirits tend to group themselves according to their nationalities while on earth. They inhabit cities and villages corresponding to those they knew in the flesh, but these places are purified and ennobled. There is no overcrowding, no slums, and no grime, and gone is every semblance of prison, asylum, workhouse, and gin palace.

Certain animals survive and find their place in the third sphere, so we learn. These creatures, however, do not live for ever. They are there for those spirits who loved them while on earth and still need their companionship. The majority of these animals are dogs, cats, horses, and a few monkeys. All have been attuned to their spirit state. Birds are part of the natural scene; in the higher spheres they glitter like precious metals, shot through with vivid colours.

The work done in the third sphere is all constructive. There is unlimited scope for artists, musicians, and all concerned to promote beauty and happiness. Teaching forms a particularly large profession. Newcomers whose minds are still occupied with the professional problems that engaged them while on earth continue for a time their special lines of inquiry. This applies especially to electrical engineering. Should they discover new knowledge they try to communicate it to those on earth by impressing it upon the minds of suitable men and women.

Occasionally those newly arrived in the third sphere are permitted to enter the seventh and there see Christ. This appears to be part of their preparation for life in the higher spheres.

Communication in the spirit world is by thought and not by language. Thus every spirit, no matter what his nationality, may communicate with all whom he meets in his new state. Drayton Thomas was told that his father enjoyed heart-to-heart talks with Cardinals, Luther and Wesley.

Drayton Thomas's father expressly repudiates the doctrine of eternal punishment. Every spirit is given the opportunity to progress, and eventually all will progress. There is no Satan, no malignant force of personal evil directing wrong-doing, either in the spirit world or on earth. One punishment for sin, besides the limiting of the etheric body, is to re-enact the evil done on earth. For those who have attained the heaven of heavens in the seventh sphere there is no punishment, though even here some of the spirits make voluntary sacrifice to neutralise or wipe out evil.

"On passing from earth," Drayton Thomas's father said in one of his most striking communications, "I realised my expectation of feeling a consciousness of God. One's God-consciousness is increased; it is clearer and He seems nearer, as I had anticipated—a part of Him, a small part."

It is possible to argue cogently that Stainton Moses's concepts of life in the hereafter may have sprung from a hidden layer of his subconsciousness. He was his own medium and he wrote "automatically". But one cannot account for the messages to Drayton Thomas in this way. The communications were passed to him through an independent medium, Mrs. Osborne Leonard. There is certainly a suggestion of the gentler Nonconformity about the Rev. Drayton Thomas's book, but no more so than its atmosphere of a spiritual Utopia such as Morris's "Nowhere" or that "Crystal Age" described by W. H. Hudson. It is for me a stretching of the "telepathy" theory to breaking point to argue that the communications passed to the sitter by Mrs. Leonard were a reflection by the medium of some hidden aspect of the sitter's mind. Nor can I accept it as likely that Mrs. Leonard invented the messages spontaneously in response to the promptings of his eager questions, presenting what she sensed would be acceptable to him and drawing from her stores of general and occult reading. I accept unhesitatingly the *bona fides* of both the Rev. Drayton Thomas and his famous medium. There is nothing whatever in his account of his long, exhaustive sittings that arouses any shadow of doubt in my mind that all was done honestly and in complete good faith. But that does not imply that I accept the communications that Mr. Drayton Thomas received through Mrs. Leonard as coming from the world of spirit. I am not convinced that they did. But how they originated I do not presume to say. I can offer no explanation.

It is rewarding to compare the theological content of *Spirit Teachings* and *Life Beyond Death* with the lecture given by the Dean of St. Paul's, Dr. W. R. Matthews, to the Society for Psychical Research in 1940. Dr. Matthews's subject was "Psychical Research and Theology". It was not Spiritualism of which he treated, but psychical research, and he limited himself to Christian theology as distinct from religion. Nevertheless it was highly significant that a man of Dr. Matthews's standing in the Anglican Church should thus lecture to the S.P.R., because as he himself emphasised the attitude of orthodox Christianity to psychical research in the past has been on the whole antagonistic, or at least suspicious. "This has not been, in the main, due to scepticism concerning the phenomena which are the subject matter of the inquiry," Dr. Matthews said, "but rather to a conviction that they were real and that they came from a source only too well known." That source was supposed to be the powers of evil.

At the outset of his lecture the Dean said that many members of the Archbishops' Commission on the claims of Spiritualism in relation to the Christian faith had been surprised by the evidence they found of the number of people who had discovered in psychical research a confirmation of their Christian faith and even been won by it from agnosticism to belief. Dr. Matthews, however, confessed that to his mind the "sermons" of the dead alleged to have been communicated mediumistically seemed, with few exceptions, more dogmatic and less coherent than those of living preachers. "We do not know," he continued, "what opportunities the alleged communicator has for arriving at a rational conclusion. Nor again, so far as I have been able to judge, is there any unanimity in the utterances of 'spirits', either on the nature of God or even on His reality. Even if we accept the spiritistic hypothesis, there is nothing of any importance to be gained with respect to belief in God from the testimony of the departed."

Dr. Matthews made it clear that he did not think psychical research offered a disproof of materialism, nor that it could do so. What psychical research has accomplished, in his opinion, is to accumulate a body of evidence that suggests, on the whole, that materialism is an inadequate theory. Spiritual and mental healing, he pointed out, the study of split personalities, clairvoyance, telekinesis, have contributed to a strengthening of contemporary conviction that the limits of what is credible were drawn too narrowly by the older rationalists. The S.P.R., in Dr. Matthews's opinion, is a standing refutation of Hume's classical argument against miracles. Hume defined a miracle as an event contrary to common experience. He argued therefore that it is more probable that testimony should be false or mistaken than that a miracle should happen. "But all the phenomena that our Society investigates," Dr. Matthews pointed out, "are contrary to common experience, yet we are persuaded that some at least of them occur."

The Dean of St. Paul's then posed the question of whether psychical research has produced any evidence which makes belief in survival more probable, from a strictly scientific point of view. He admitted the black record of deceit, fraud, and illusion which condemns so much of past psychic research. But after making every allowance for this he expressed the opinion that there remains a core of established facts which, *prima facie,* suggests the hypothesis of survival. He ended his lecture with this expression of his own attitude:

"Personal survival is the hypothesis that the centre of consciousness which was in existence before death does not cease to be in existence after death and that the experience of this centre after death has the same kind of continuity with its experience before death as that of a man who sleeps for a while and wakes again. The difficulty that our experience is largely that of states and changes of our bodies is certainly formidable but not, I think, decisive. We have at least in Professor Prince's Presidential Address some valuable suggestions towards the conception of a 'spiritual body' which has a real continuity with the body of flesh. I repeat, the survival hypothesis may be hard to accept, but I cannot think it is hard to understand."

There is thus a wide gulf between Dr. Matthews, the Dean of St. Paul's, who is a "psychical researcher", and such Spiritualists as Stainton Moses and the Rev. Drayton Thomas. Dr. Matthews is tentative, hesitant, and critical. Moses and Thomas are confident, dogmatic, and convinced. But wide though the gulf is, it separates men who are moving in the same direction. They are allies, not enemies. Much has still to be done, theologically, metaphysically, and scientifically before the gulf is firmly bridged. Even so, the concepts of heaven and hell have been reinstated as worthy of credence by twentieth-century men and women. That has followed inevitably the strengthening belief in survival after death, a belief held by orthodox Christians and Spiritualists alike. Our image of those future states has changed considerably, but conviction of their reality is firm and genuine. Milton's vision has been rekindled:

> *Millions of spiritual creatures walk the Earth*
> *Unseen, both when we wake, and when we sleep . . .*
> *What if earth and heaven be to each other like*
> *More than on earth is thought?*

CHAPTER VI

A SPIRITUALIST SERVICE

HAD the choice been mine I would not have gone out that Sunday evening. It was cold and damp, and the wind was snell. The fireside was strongly attractive. But I had arranged to attend my first service at a Spiritualist church, and I forced myself to make the effort.

Not everyone shared my reluctance to be abroad that night. Kingsway, the main link between the Strand and Euston, was thronged. Many turned in at Kingsway Hall, a famous Methodist meeting-place, but I hurried on and found that Bloomsbury Square was crowded with parked motor-cars. There I entered a towering insurance building, and was carried by the throng downstairs. There is a hall in the basement where the Marylebone Spiritualist Association holds an open, non-sectarian service every Sunday evening. The M.S.A. has no other church or chapel, although around London and in many provincial towns Spiritualist churches have been established, and even equipped with organs. Spiritualists, I have come to learn, have a special fondness for organ music, but neither this nor even a chapel is essential to the practice of their faith. They are equally at home in the Royal Albert Hall or a small suburban parlour when conducting their religion.

Any stranger who ventures to join for the first time a religious service he has previously heard of only at second hand must be a little uneasy and anxious to guard against social solecisms. It is the lot of a journalist, such as I, to attend a large number of religious ceremonies. In time you learn to adapt yourself to the various proprieties—not to remove your hat, for example, in a synagogue and to take off your shoes in a mosque. But a Spiritualist service presented—

or seemed to present—a range of new problems. How does one act, I wondered, in the company of ghosts? I imagined that spirits would be conjured from another world for the benefit of this congregation, and I was unsure how my nerves would stand their appearance. What I associate with ghosts are churchyards and ruined castles at midnight, clanking chains, the smell of mould, *Hamlet,* and the synthetic eeriness of stories in Christmas numbers. None of this was apparent in the hall where I now found myself. Instead, a school prize-giving might have been about to take place, or an amateur dramatic society preparing to perform *Bunty Pulls The Strings.* The gathering was as matter-of-fact, as homely, and as intimate as that.

The congregation numbered about 500. This, I was told, was about the average at one of these Sunday-evening services of the M.S.A. For an organisation whose membership is around 7,000 this did not strike me as a particularly high proportion, but it is no worse than the run of most parish churches, and a good deal better than some. And, after all, the membership of the M.S.A. is not localised but extremely scattered. There were more women than men in the gathering, and more older people than girls and young men, just as there are in most congregations of whatever denomination. For the most part they looked comfortable rather than well-to-do people. Perhaps the bulk of them came from a little below the middle Middle Class, but there was plainly a mixture of people from many social levels, just as there is in most church or chapel congregations.

The first fact I noticed to set this gathering apart from most religious congregations was that those people in the front of the hall were sitting in reserved seats for which they had paid 2s. 6d. each, though members and associates of the M.S.A. had paid a little less. Behind this phalanx were the free seats, for which a silver collection was taken at the door. On entering, a hymn-book was handed to everyone, and though there was no choir there was music from a grand piano to accompany the singing. Some services have both piano and organ playing together. The congregation was well served by sidesmen and women. On the stage at the far end of the hall were two microphones—a modern touch. In front of the stage were two large vases of flowers, and on either side were palms in pots. The hall was flooded with bright electric light which shone back from the many chromed fittings in the room. There was here no "dim religious light", no stained glass and flickering candle flames. Instead was a cheerful, though secular, brightness.

While we waited for the service to begin a young woman played some Schubert on the piano. She shyly announced her own programme. I studied the faces of those in the congregation and was struck by the happiness of their expression. I suppose that subconsciously I had been assuming that Spiritualism must make its strongest appeal to those who have lately suffered a poignant bereavement. But those around me were not mourners. They were not grieving. Just as, thirty years earlier, the abiding impression J. B. Rhine had carried away from a lecture given in Chicago by Sir Arthur Conan Doyle had been of the supreme happiness his belief had inspired in the speaker, so I in my turn at my initial experience of Spiritualism at first hand had borne into my mind quite powerfully the same conviction that, whatever else it may do, this creed does banish sorrow.

In an earlier chapter I have named the seven fundamental principles on which the greater part of Spiritualist churches base their teaching. These principles are essentially religious, but in public gatherings they are taken for granted. No one is normally called upon to affirm them. At these Spiritualist services there is no recital of a creed, no litany, no solemn ritual. Nor is there anyone to conduct the service analogous to a clergyman. A chairman—who is often a woman—presides. That is all. There are no deacons and other lay officials.

During that first service I am describing we sang two hymns from the Spiritualists' hymn-book. Sometimes four hymns are called for. There was a reading from the New Testament. A soloist sang Handel's *Where'er You Walk* and two simple ballads, and we were given a twenty-minute address on Spiritualism by a practised speaker. He wore a brown suit and a burgundy-coloured pullover, and his talk or sermon, call it what you will, was as informal as his clothes. But he knew how to hold an audience, how to speak into a microphone, and how to use his hands. He attempted no profundities, but told how he himself had discovered the "fact" of survival and of the "richer, fuller, healthier life" it assured all human beings when they have passed through "that state we miscall death". He referred to the prejudice and fear surrounding Spiritualism which have made it a barred subject with many people, and he stressed the comfort and consolation it offers.

And so we moved to the climax of the evening—a demonstration of clairvoyance to prove, said the chairwoman, the fact of survival.

The medium came forward to the front of the stage and stationed herself beside one of the microphones. The lights remained at full blaze. She was a tall woman who wore a blouse of deep green and a black skirt. She pointed down the hall. "I have a message for two ladies just where I am pointing," she said.

The effect was electrical. The attention of the whole congregation became concentrated. Everyone was rapt, tense, completely absorbed. All leaned forward in their seats, so eager they were to catch all that was said. The medium had many messages to give. She spoke rapidly and with a sort of nervous impatience. It seemed to me that she was listening with one half of her brain while speaking with the other half—receiving and transmitting, as it were, at the same time. She was receiving, we were to believe, messages from the world of spirit and transmitting these to men and women in the congregation. Occasionally she shut her eyes. Now and then she talked half-audibly to herself. "Yes, yes, I will tell them," I heard her say once. The congregation appeared to have no doubt that she was communing with the spirit world.

A Welshwoman was told that she and her daughter, to their surprise and delight, would soon go back to live in a house in

Brook Road or Brook Street, Cardiff. The address had meaning for them, but they were certain that they had no prospect of removing at present. No matter, the spirits knew better. Bert, an electrician, who is working "above water", was warned to take the utmost care because "you are specially valuable at home and cannot be spared. Does that mean anything to you?" He agreed that it did.

Occasionally people were called by name, though as a rule the medium pointed to different parts of the hall and then gave clues by which members of the congregation were able to identify whether the message was for them. Once or twice the message, when it was delivered, puzzled its recipient. But the medium was not to be put off. "No, I won't take that back—it is important," she insisted. There was nothing solemn about the proceedings. The medium kept up a succession of little jokes which aroused the congregation to much laughter.

On the whole the messages seemed to me to incline to the trivial, though I admit the congregation did not appear to rate them so. "Someone is trying desperately to come in," the medium mentioned at one point, but when the spirit's identity had been established to the satisfaction of a woman in the hall, the message that he was so anxious to send was this: "He says you have a neighbour who has been quarrelling. Does that mean anything? It does? You are to go to her at once and tell her to hold her tongue and not be such a fool. That is very urgent."

Another woman admitted she had not been able to bring herself to go through her dead mother's possessions. "When you do you will get a pleasant surprise," the medium said, "because your mother is showing me a ten-shilling note. On the earth plane she used to wear a scarf round her neck in a special way and a feather ornament in her hat. Do you agree?"

For still another woman there was a message from a blind man. "He says he is very happy," the medium announced. "He is saying, 'Let me get at my old woman.' It's a joke—he never called you that on the earth plane. Have you looked at his watch lately? No? Then I want you to look at it tonight.

Its hands point to twelve minutes past twelve. I am telling you that to prove that the spirit people can see inside drawers."

Then a boy named Ronnie "broke in", according to the medium. "He would be about so high," she said, indicating with her hand. "He died from meningitis or a head complaint. Knocked down, was he? He wants me to remind you of the little cart with two dappled horses he was so proud of when you used to push him in it. By now he would have been about thirty years of age. You keep a flower in a vase before a photograph of him. 'I promise you, mother,' he is saying, 'you will not be alone at Christmas.' He tells me that you talk to him a lot. You never miss saying 'Good morning' and 'Good night' to him. Is that so?" To me that was the most pathetic revelation of the evening.

No one contradicted the medium on any material point, though sometimes she was corrected on points of detail. She said, for example, that the watch with the hands standing at twelve minutes past twelve was a gold one, and was told 'it was of silver. Except for the putting right of such details, there were no denials.

That was the first demonstration of clairvoyance I had ever seen. Did the medium talk, as she asserted that she did, with the spirits of the dead, or had she some extraordinary gift of telepathy, if you like, that enabled her to read the thoughts of people in the congregation? I do not know the answer, but it is strongly denied by Spiritualists that telepathy is the explanation. If you question them on this possibility they will supply numerous instances of messages received that could not possibly have been a reflection of the recipient's mind because they referred to matters of which those for whom they were intended had no cognisance until later. Nevertheless the latest study of telepathy has suggested the possibility that it may be independent of time so that those who have this power strongly developed may be able to foretell future states of mind. I confess I am at a loss to explain how the phenomenon of clairvoyance comes about, but I am completely satisfied that the congregation at the service I have described accepted without a shadow of doubt the medium's complete honesty, and they, of course, were versed in Spiritualistic practice and would, I believe, have been quick to detect trickery had there been any.

At the end of half an hour the demonstration was snapped off as though a switch had been flicked. Time was up. The medium looked exhausted as she went back to her chair on the stage. I handed my hymn-book to a steward and followed the congregation upstairs and out into the wintry darkness of Bloomsbury Square. Though I had seen no ghosts, I had more than enough to think about.

An epilogue is necessary to this chapter. Six months later I attended another Spiritualist service in the same hall. It was merely a whim that took me there, coupled to a vague wish to watch another medium at work. It so happened that the advertised medium met with an accident as he stepped from the train on his way to the service. He was detained in hospital, and so at the last minute a substitute had to be found. It proved to be the clairvoyant I had first seen, and so I was able to compare her demonstration with the earlier one. It occurred to me that if there was any collusion, any faking or trickery, it would betray itself by a repetition of certain effects. I hasten to say that I discerned not even a hint of such a repetition.

The differences between the two services were on matters of detail only. Four hymns were sung instead of the previous two. There was a short period of silent prayer, an Invocation, two Bible readings, the chanting of the Lord's Prayer, a short effective address defining the essentials of the Spiritualist's faith and on what these are based which was given by the secretary of the M.S.A., Mr. Ralph Rossiter, and finally the demonstration of clairvoyance.

The medium had, she said, a message from an old gentleman. She judged his age to be about seventy. "He has not been long in spirit," she explained. "When he died he had something the matter with his chest, because he had great difficulty in getting his breath. He says he can now breathe again. He had to go down a flight of steps to enter his house —I suppose it was a basement flat. He keeps pointing to those steps and saying, 'Tell her to be careful.'" The member of the audience who identified the message said that it came from a man who had fallen down a flight of steps about a year before his death. "He is tremendously excited," the medium went on. "He keeps saying, 'Tell them I am sorry I was such a nuisance before I passed over. It is all right now.'"

One message was from a man specifically named Pearson —Alf or Alfred Pearson. "It is for someone named Edith, level with my hand," the medium explained. "You say it is for you, madam? Will you hold up your hand, please, so that I can know where you are? Without my glasses I can see only a blur of faces. Have you a link with the police? Yes? Is it a relative, please?"

"No, it is my husband," was the reply, and this elicited a ripple of laughter.

"I am receiving a message from your mother," the medium continued. "She says that at first she did not approve of your choice of a husband, but that now she takes it all back. She says she has become very fond of your husband. Has he retired lately? Is he looking for a job, please?"

"Well, he does study the newspaper a lot," was the wary reply, which again caused laughter.

"Then you can tell him this: Alf Pearson, who was with him in the police, is bringing forward a fine Alsatian dog and he says your husband should breed dogs. Will you give him that message? Thank you."

There was a little confusion when the medium announced she had a message for a twin. Two women in different parts of the hall said they had twin sisters. At first the medium thought that the message was for the twin on her left, but when this woman had denied in turn that she was the elder, being in fact two hours her sister's junior, that her sister was fair, that she knew someone named George, and that her father was in spirit, it became apparent that the message was not for her. The other twin on the medium's right passed all these tests.

"Your father, mother, and George are all in spirit?" she was asked.

"Yes."

"Then the message is for you. Is your twin about to remove her home?"

"I believe she is thinking of doing so."

"I am sure of it. I feel a complete change—a washing out of the past. Will you tell her, madam, that your father, mother, and George all approve of her plans. They say they will 'push her along'.

"There is a message now from someone, a man, who passed over while he was walking along a path or in a garden. He passed over quite suddenly."

A hand was held up.

"Was he your father?"

"No, my uncle."

"He wants you to know your father is with him."

"Yes, he would be."

"He was an extremely jocular man. He says, making a joke of it, 'I died with my boots on, but they did not kick me out of heaven.'"

"I understand that."

"What important anniversary have you this month?"

"I don't know. I can't think of one. Oh yes, of course, it is my mother's birthday."

"She is showing me a beautiful bouquet of white flowers."

"I know what that means."

"Who is Rose?"

"That was my mother's name. And it is my name too."

"What was the game that was often played at home with the children?"

"I don't know."

"It was either draughts or dominoes. Yes, it was dominoes. Have you still got the set?"

"I think so—yes, I am sure I have."

"Well, one piece is missing from the set. Did you know?"

"No, I did not."

D

"I can tell you that the missing piece is the 6-4. When you get home will you examine the set and let me know, please, if that piece is missing."

"Yes, I certainly will."

But now it was almost eight o'clock and the hall had to be cleared. The demonstration was over. The chairman said it was one of the most brilliant examples of clairvoyance he had ever known that medium give. I can well believe it. Perhaps because it did not tally with my preconceived notions of what the dead would communicate to those they loved on earth if a channel were opened to them I still could not—and cannot even yet—bring myself to believe that it proved the "fact" of survival. I accept the phenomenon of clairvoyance, as I think all must do who have examined the impressive body of evidence concerning it that investigators of every kind have accumulated, but I cannot explain it. I doubt if telepathy is the explanation, though an element of telepathy may be associated with it. Those who do accept such demonstrations as these as proof of survival have my respect and sympathy. I do not dismiss them as gullible and credulous. But my own attitude is that of one still open to conviction.

In discussions I have had with Spiritualists concerning clairvoyance I have been told that not every medium who is a good demonstrator in public is equally effective at private sittings. It is said that with a large audience the clairvoyant is able to choose among the many "spirit people" he is aware of hovering, as it were, among the congregation and concentrate on those who are strongest to him. Contrariwise, those who are specially successful at private sittings may be ineffective on a platform because of shyness and lack of confidence. It is very easy, I am told, for a medium to become disconcerted when passing on a message that appears to be nonsense to the person who receives it. The mediums, so it was emphasised to me, are but the instruments of those who have passed over and are used by the spirits as they please. Mediums cannot be expected to interpret the messages they pass. It is for the recipients to examine these and interpret their significance. Despite these reservations, there are many mediums who are equally successful in public and in private. Any medium who obtains results, whether in the seance room or on the platform, that are better than average is quickly known throughout the movement and is at once besieged with requests for sittings, so hungry are the rank-and-file for certainty.

And now I must report on my own experience of sitting in private with mediums.

CHAPTER VII

MEDIUMS AND THEIR WORK

EDIUMS are absolutely essential to the practice of
Spiritualism. At a pinch Christianity can do without
clergymen, and indeed in one sect of it, the Society
of Friends, it is part of the persuasion to dispense with them.
But Spiritualism, although essentially a branch of Christianity,
breaks down completely without mediums, because there is
no other means of bridging the gulf between the physical
world and the world of spirit. Mediums are held to be links
in a system of communication and are analogous to telephones
and radio sets. They do, in fact, often speak of working on
certain vibrations, and if the "frequencies" emanating from the
Spiritual World are outside their range then there is no
message, no communication. To my mind it is a weakness in
the Spiritualists' presentation of their case that they are content
to use these rough-and-ready analogies which raise as many
difficulties as they surmount. Mediums are channels of communication whether they are clairvoyants, healers, psychome-
tricians (people who can "read" objects that the dead once
possessed as the blind "read" Braille), or the materialisers of
physical phenomena out of the spirit world. It follows, therefore, that Spiritualism is absolutely dependent on the integrity
of its mediums. If that integrity becomes tarnished by even
the slightest breath of fraud, then the cause is gravely damaged,
and a series of exposures, following each other in rapid succession, could easily damage the movement beyond recovery.

That fraud is practised by some mediums is admitted both
by Spiritualists and their critics. The movement is at pains to
ensure that its mediums are above suspicion. It incites them
to develop their powers, and it warns them repeatedly that
these are in danger of being impaired if they are used too

frequently. The temptation to strain their mediumship is a strong one, for most mediums earn their living by means of the rare faculty with which they have been born and have laboriously developed. It becomes difficult to refuse sittings and thus turn away money, and as a medium's reputation grows so the public begin to clamour for his services, and persons of wealth and fame bid high for the experience of sitting with him. A medium, therefore, must be someone of strong character if he is to refuse to exhaust his powers. Yet if those powers are exhausted, then more than ever he will be tempted to fake results so as to obtain bread. He becomes a conjuror masquerading as a medium. Against these abuses a constant watch is kept, as I have earlier described, by the leaders of the movement.

Yet even if Spiritualists contrive to keep their house in strict order, they are powerless against the charlatan outside their movement. Anyone who chooses to can set up as a medium and call himself a Spiritualist. If he is shown up as an impostor, he pulls down in his fall part of the jealously guarded reputation of Spiritualism.

Though Spiritualists readily admit the presence of fraud, they are not all agreed about the culprits. An instance of this is the fate of Mrs. Helen Duncan. She was born at Callander, Perthshire, in 1898, married a working man in Glasgow, and became the mother of six children. In 1931 there was some controversy in London over her mediumship. Two years later she was convicted in Edinburgh for obtaining £4 from sitters by false pretences, and for this she was fined £10. She continued, however, to practise mediumship, and during the war she was in such demand that she could ask £104 for a week's engagement in Portsmouth. Up to 12s. 6d. was charged for a seat at one of her seances. All this was stated at her trial at the Old Bailey in March 1944, and a police witness added that despite these fees Mrs. Duncan had paid no income tax. She was prosecuted under the unrepealed Witchcraft Act, found guilty, and sent to prison for nine months. Her case was taken to the Court of Appeal, but the verdict and the sentence were

upheld. Many Spiritualists of unquestioned probity gave
evidence on Mrs. Duncan's behalf during her trial. The defence
offered to demonstrate her powers to the jury, but this was
not allowed. It is still maintained by a substantial number of
Spiritualists that Mrs. Duncan was martyrised. Despite this,
I should think that few unprejudiced readers can read through
the verbatim report of the trial, published in the *Notable
British Trials* series, without agreeing that the evidence against
Mrs. Duncan was strong.

An instance of the damage that can be done to Spiritualism
by an impostor outside the movement is that of Charles
Botham, who was convicted on June 20, 1950, on three counts
of false pretences. There were also two counts of conjuration
under the Witchcraft Act, but these two counts were never
presented to the court and the jury were discharged from
returning a verdict upon them. Botham was said, so Mr.
Chuter Ede told the House of Commons, to have persuaded
a widow to place sums of money, amounting to £1,000 and
£500, on a chair so that the spirit of her late husband could
dematerialise them and apply them to medical charities. "The
notes were not dematerialised, but, in a very material form,
reached Mr. Botham's wallet," Mr. Ede declared. The jury's
verdict affirmed their conviction that the "seance" was a fraud.

Since the Fraudulent Mediums Act, 1951, became law a
medium has been prosecuted under its provisions. The London
magistrate who heard the charge declined to send the case for
trial and discharged the medium after hearing the defence.

My own experience of mediums is limited to sittings with
seven of them, and of watching, what I shall describe later,
three sessions with Spiritualist "healers". All the mediums
with whom I sat were clairvoyants and they were nominated
by the Marylebone Spiritualist Association. I sat with no
"physical" mediums, as those are called who produce spirit
materialisations and talk in the Direct Voice through a mega-
phone. This was because I heard of none who would be willing
to sit for me under test conditions. It seemed to me that seven
clairvoyants ought to provide a fair sample. All the same, it

is a characteristic of avowed Spiritualists that they go from medium to medium, restlessly searching for the revelation, which seems always to elude them, that would persuade them with the blinding certainty that was Paul's on the road to Damascus. The appearance of a medium of startlingly new technique excites interest throughout the movement.

I learned nothing from my mediums that convinced me beyond doubt that they were receiving messages from the spirit world to prove the continuity of life after the body's death. Nothing happened at these sittings to make me doubt the integrity of these mediums. I will go further and say that some of them attracted me by their modesty and what I took to be their sincerity. Even so, at the end of the series I was conscious that the intellectual elation I felt after attending my first Spiritualist service had lost some of its buoyancy and had begun to sag a little.

The Marylebone Spiritual Association had warned me of this before I began my sittings. They told me that it might well be that all seven seances would prove entirely negative. If that happened they offered to arrange another series for me, and, if necessary and I was still willing to go on, another series after that.

"It is not easy to get good results at first," I was told. "Communication between the spirit world and the earth plane depends on vibrations, and to 'tune in' to these the medium has, as it were, to pick up the right wavelength. Not every wireless set is made to pick up short-wave radio signals. Similarly, not every medium is able to tune in to the required messages. The messages are there, just as the radio signals are in the ether, but the spirit cannot get through because the medium is not tuned in to receive them."

I was asked always to remember that even the best mediums are liable to make mistakes. All statements that are contrary to known facts should be rejected, I was told, and any advice which conflicted with good sense should be probed further.

The brochure published by the Marylebone Spiritualist Association contains these Notes for the Guidance of

Investigators: "Mediums respond to a sincere and friendly approach. To deceive or to adopt a blatantly sceptical attitude is a great mistake and is likely to result in provoking false or ridiculous information. The difficulties in defining absolute proof of survival are apparent; it is for each investigator carefully to weigh the evidence and to decide whether a supernormal source alone can be responsible.

"Every interview is an experiment. Mediums cannot command results, they can only pass on what they receive, often with some difficulty and confusion. It is unwise to press a medium for any particular piece of information or to gain contact with any particular individual who has passed over.

"Nevertheless the Council believe that investigators who patiently and persistently pursue their enquiries, making due allowance for the complexity of the subject and innumerable obstacles that obstruct the path, must eventually reach the conviction attained by so many during the eighty-odd years of our existence—that human personality survives death."

It is noteworthy that the Rev. C. Drayton Thomas, after an experience of seances extending over more than twenty-two years, came to believe that scepticism did not make any appreciable difference to the success of a sitting if the manner was polite, tactful and kindly, the sitter was receptive, and did not concentrate on confirming his prejudices.

While I believe that I for my part co-operated with the mediums in the way these Notes called for, and that the mediums strove all they knew to supply me with some "evidence" that could have come to them only by supernatural means, yet at the end of the sittings I was still unsatisfied. I had received no jolt, been given none of the startling revelations of intimate family happenings such as so many Spiritualists recount with awe, enthusiasm, and wonderment. All seven "sets", it seemed, were not tuned to the requisite wavelength.

Now I am willing to admit that a sitter desperately anxious for a sign that this world and the other are linked and that communication between the two is possible might be so overwhelmed by no more than I was told by my mediums that unshakable conviction would follow. The will to believe would be there, so that acceptance of the "evidence" would be readier than it is, I confess, with me.

At this point Spiritualists will charge me, I suppose, with stubborn scepticism. I do not admit this. I was sitting with the mediums as an inquirer, it is true, but one who was prejudiced, if at all, in favour of the Spiritualist hypothesis, but so trained, or should I say "enmeshed", in a habit of thinking that I cannot readily accept evidence at its face value. I do not pocket my intellectual change without first ringing it on the counter of criticism. And in one important particular I differed from most of those who are attracted to Spiritualism. My own need lacked urgency. There was no one "on the other side" from whom I hungered to have a message. Death had not lately robbed me of someone on whom all my love was lavished. I was seeking intellectual assurance rather than, as with most Spiritual novices, emotional solace.

Only two of the mediums with whom I sat were women. They were neither more nor less successful than their male colleagues. I was informed that at the M.S.A. the mediums are not told who it is that is sitting with them. A number instead of a name is given to the medium by those in the office who arrange the sitting. The aim is to ensure a certain impersonality and avoid the possibility of details being passed on as spirit messages that may after all be fairly common knowledge. The mediums disclaim all responsibility for the messages they communicate. This helps to explain what is meant by the statement in the M.S.A.'s "Notes" that "To deceive or to adopt a blatantly sceptical attitude . . . is likely to result in provoking false or ridiculous information". It is held that the spirits of the dead bitterly resent any attempt to hoodwink them, and respond by giving the medium non-sensical messages to relay to the sitter. The only censorship the mediums exercise is when by means of clairvoyance they learn something that might be dangerous or seriously upsetting for the sitter to know. Such information they refrain from conveying. Information "from the other side" comes to the medium through his spirit "guide" or "control", who may be a Chinaman who has "passed over", an Arab, a Red Indian—anyone, in fact. Except when the medium is able to practise the Direct Voice technique, by which the dead themselves are supposed to speak in tones that can be recognised as theirs, the control takes the message from the dead, and passes it to the medium who in turn relays it to the sitter. Some mediums go into a complete trance during a sitting, and then the spirit guide speaks to the sitter, using the medium's larynx, brain, and tongue for the purpose. A question frequently asked by those outside the Spiritualist movement is, Why are so many "guides" Red Indians? It is true that some famous mediums have had Red Indian guides, but Spiritualists say that the proportion is not in fact unduly large. These spirit guides are people who during their time on earth had developed their psychic gifts, either consciously or unconsciously, by living close to Nature and the Universal Essence. The way of life adopted by the Red Indians was specially favourable for the heightening of this kind of mystical exercise, so that in the "other world" they found themselves qualified to serve as links between the two worlds. But this role is not exclusively that of those who once lived as Red Indians, but is shared by people of all races, nations, and civilisations.

Two of my sittings were with trance mediums. My first experience of seeing anyone in a trance came when I was sitting with a woman medium. The room had been blacked out, but the gas fire was burning and a dim red light from an electric bulb in the centre of the room had been switched on. The medium, a comfortable, friendly little body, asked to hold both my hands. She explained that she had to wait until her control, known as Sambo, came through. "In this life he was a man with a dark skin, but not now, you understand," she said, and added that until Sambo came she would practise clairvoyance. She did not impress me as having this gift in any great strength, but on this point I may be doing her an injustice; after all, we were not together for any considerable length of time and I have never met her since, so my knowledge of her work is scanty.

After fifteen minutes or so Sambo came. His arrival was sudden, and I had no warning of what was about to happen. The medium's body grew rigid. Her grip on my hands tightened. She babbled words that were unintelligible to me. A panic feeling darted in my mind about what I should do if, in fact, the medium was having a fit. My knowledge of first aid is as beggarly as my knowledge of Spiritualism was at that time. But I had read that it can be extremely dangerous physically for a medium to be subjected to natural or artificial light while in a trance. There are, it is said, instances of mediums being blinded, disabled, or otherwise harmed by so doing. Yet how, I wondered, could I get help for this woman if she was really in a fit, and her panting breathing, the tightness of her grip upon my hands, the rigidity of her body, and the high-pitched sounds coming from her lips all suggested to my mind that she was suffering some form of epilepsy. Presently, however, the gibberish she was speaking changed to English. She, or her control, now spoke to me in what I thought was a rather unnatural voice—thinner, shriller, and more emphatic than her normal tones, but still hers though distorted.

It was the first time I had ever conversed with the spirit world—if indeed Sambo was a spirit. (Strange how this doubt intrudes itself into my reporting.) I admit I was shy. Although Sambo proved to be a fluent speaker, it was not always easy to keep the conversation going. If the discussion halted, this talkative spirit would demand whether there was not something more I wished to ask him? I confess that what seemed to me the unreality of this interview in the darkened room, sitting by a gas-fire at a card-table, or some such piece of furniture, and holding the hands of an apparently unconscious woman, made it difficult for me to think of suitable questions. And then Sambo would become impatient and hector me. He was a commanding spirit, but by no means an intimidating one. I feel that on longer acquaintance we should get on well together.

We conversed for a good twenty minutes. Sambo told me he approved of my son. "The little papoose—I like him," he said benignly, and forecast a fine future for him. "Your mother is here and watching," Sambo continued. "She too likes the little papoose. She tells me she often bends over him while he is in his cot. She is very fond of him—oh, very fond of him indeed."

Sambo warned me that my blood stream was not in order and that I must be careful about it, but that the malady was nothing serious and could easily be put right. If Sambo wished to stress a point in what he was telling me he would use the medium's hands to pull on mine. The grip was stronger than I should have expected from the plump little medium.

When the conversation ended and Sambo departed, the medium slowly relaxed. She screwed up her eyes and the muscles of her face twitched. Slowly she awakened. She shivered as though with cold.

"I always know when Sambo has been," she said, speaking now in her natural voice. "I feel so very much bigger. Of course, I don't know what is said while I am in trance."

In the course of my sittings I heard of "sickness lights", of maps dotted with flags, of old bearded gentlemen in smoking caps, and a succession of more or less common Christian names, such as Mary, John, William, and Anne or Hannah, none of which, oddly enough, are those of people at all close to me. One sitting took place in the broad light of afternoon. The curtains were not drawn, so that I could see from where I sat a tall slender tree in the garden. This medium told me that his father had been a Roman Catholic and that two of his uncles were priests, but his mother had been the daughter of a Church of England clergyman and that he himself had been intended for the Anglican Church. He had been a medium since he was fourteen years of age. I estimate his age at the time of the sitting to have been about forty-four. He told me he believed fervently in a future life. There was not the slightest doubt, he asserted, that survival had been established irrefutably.

"You are psychic," he told me. "I see you as the centre of intense spiritual activity. Your brother who died in infancy is your Guardian Angel. The work you do is strenuous and bustling. I hear in the distance the sound of great machines. I see many typewriters—a pouring out of type.

"On your father's side I see a spirit aged about fifty-eight who had been ill but died unexpectedly. I think he was a Freemason, for I see a Masonic sign of two triangles. On your mother's side I see a lady in late middle age who was older than she looked. Her appearance is very regal, but for all that she was exceptionally kind-hearted. Her name was Anne, or Hannah. There is someone else connected with her called Mary Anne. A lady who is close to you is ill, but not seriously. It is some stomach or internal trouble. If it is suggested that she should have an operation I would advise against it, because such an operation would set up complications later.

"You have travelled extensively," (this was eminently true) "and are about to do so again. I see a board room with the directors in session. Over it is a flag. This board is possibly connected in some way with Government. There is to be a considerable branching out in activity for you. It is in the nature of promotion and will bring increased responsibilities. The spirits approve that you should undertake this work.

"I am now getting an empty stage. Someone you know connected with the stage has lately passed over. There is also a prison camp, a Japanese camp. Someone about twenty-eight years of age died in it. There is a strong link here with some people named Hunter."

Nothing that was told me during that sitting seemed to bear upon my own life either past, present, or future, apart from the early reference to type, typewriters, and large machines, for I work in a newspaper office. I find it curious that although most of the mediums approached the subject of my work in this tentative way, not one of them made the plain statement that I am a journalist by profession. I do not understand this shyness or timidity. The reference to the empty stage impressed me. To the best of my knowledge I have only one friend who works in the theatre. She is a ballet dancer. Because I had not heard from her for some time I rang her up soon after leaving the sitting. She was very much alive.

A medium who told me he worked in trance showed none of the symptoms displayed by his woman colleague while under the guidance of Sambo. The seance room was darkened by drawing heavy curtains. Again a dim red light was switched on. We did not hold hands, but sat about three feet apart on either side of the gas-fire. The medium appeared to concentrate intensely. He spoke throughout the sitting in his normal voice.

"On your mother's side," he said, "perhaps two generations back, is a lady named Elizabeth or Eliza, and she is calling, 'Sam, Sam.'"

"That was my father's name," I told him.

"I see the sea, and mountains. This means that Elizabeth either lived beside the sea in mountainous country or else that she came to England from abroad. Over you is the initial M. I get 'Sam, Sam' insistently and 'David'. The sea and the mountains are most clear.

"There is a big change coming for you in your work. Connected with it is someone named Phillips."

Suddenly the medium shrugged his shoulders and opened his arms in a gesture of despair. We had been sitting for less than a quarter of an hour. He got up and drew back the curtains, letting in the light.

"I can't go on," he said. "It is useless. I should be guessing and would mislead you. I am not getting through. But there is one thing unconnected with the spirit world I must tell you. I see a large book. Someone is turning over the pages. He comes to a blank page—a page with no writing. A chapter in your life is ending."

I thanked him for his honesty in cutting short the seance. It was one of the incidents that impressed me most throughout the series of sittings. But again nothing had been mentioned that seemed to touch directly on my life apart from mentioning a name that had been my father's.

Among the best hits achieved by the mediums was to say that I had very strong links with South Africa. I have in fact a brother in Johannesburg and an aunt in Cape Town.

One medium described accurately the deaths of my parents. Another said excitedly he had a message for Rogers or Roger. "Roger" is my boy's name. I was told unhesitatingly that my parents had four children, and then the medium spoiled the effect by saying that one of these children was a girl. We were four brothers. Once, all unwittingly, I may have misled one of the seven. She stated vehemently that I have an important anniversary in August. Just as vehemently I denied it. She was distinctly nonplussed and pressed me whether I was certain that the month of August is completely unmarked in my calendar. I held to it that to the best of my recollection no event of any importance in my life has taken place in August. But in this I was wrong. I cannot account for this aberration. No woman would have made the mistake I made then. It was not until days later that I remembered my wedding anniversary is in August. . . .

One medium described me as some sort of artist. "You express yourself through your hands, though you are neither a musician nor a painter," he said. "You have a profession of some sort, though I cannot exactly place it. You work amidst a lot of people. Go on doing as you are now, and a great success will be yours in a year or two.

"When you leave the seance room you will go to a place where there is always incessant movement. You do not rest enough. Rest is very necessary.

"Who is Leslie?" he demanded, breaking off his rapid flow of talk. I told him I had had a brother named Leslie who had died as a young man.

"He is very near to you," the medium said. "You are one of three brothers," (four would have been correct). "I do not see your mother. But your brother and your father are present. What is the link with South Africa?"

The way in which South Africa was so often repeated to me was, by itself, impressive. One medium prophesied that

I was soon to travel to Gambia—a curious place to pick on. I am still waiting to make that journey.

How did the mediums know so much that was correct? Was it spirit communication, telepathy, inspired guessing, or what? I confess I do not know.

Where they definitely went wrong was over my astrological sign, saying that my family are farmers, that someone named Ruth is very close to me, and that my father was a practical man who liked talking politics. I was told repeatedly, and I confess I found it flattering, that I am extremely psychic and possess unusual powers of healing.

As I have said, many sitters would, I am sure, have found much of the detail given strongly convincing. I was left unsatisfied, because two facts that to my mind are all-important were never mentioned. One was the reluctance, if that is what it was, to state my occupation. The other was that my boy, Roger, is an adopted child. They never even got to hinting at that. Somehow their power could not penetrate that far.

If my recollection is accurate, I began each sitting by asking the mediums how I could best co-operate with them. They asked me to relax, to put anxiety from my mind, and to tell them whenever they were passing accurate information to me. These things I tried to do to the best of my ability. And there were times in the sittings when I let my mind concentrate on some fact connected with my work or home which I hoped the medium would pass back to me. This would, of course, have been no more than a suggestion of telepathy, but in no instance did the medium speak to me of these facts, such as my brother's name or the writing I was engaged on.

Nevertheless I believe I did establish a certain sympathy with some, at any rate, of the mediums, because of the confidences they made to me. One medium, for example, volunteered to tell me how his mother had died. He had been told one Christmas that she would not live for more than a few hours. He sat up with her, and about 2 a.m. he gave her a sleeping tablet which the doctor had left. "Now go to sleep, mother, and we will have a talk in the morning," he told her. She never woke. Some time later he mentioned to his wife that he believed his mother knew she was dying when he gave her the tablet. Weeks afterwards his wife sat, unknown to him, with a medium in the town where they lived. The medium gave her a message from her mother-in-law. "Tell Fred," she said, "I knew I was going to die, but I did not say anything." He then made this comment to me which he uttered with extreme conviction: "I *know* there is no death as we understand it."

Although I sat with no physical mediums, I did hear Alder-man Evan Powell, of Paignton, plead in a lecture for more physical mediumship these days. In Chapter II I gave Sir Arthur Conan Doyle's opinion of Mr. Powell's mediumship and his reputation is extraordinarily high. His control, Black Hawk, a six-foot North American Indian, is known through-out the movement. Alderman Evan Powell is now in his seventies and no longer takes sittings. In his heyday he was one of the greatest of physical mediums.

"Each generation of Spiritualists wants proof that will hit it in the eye," he said. "Physical manifestations are still needed, just as much as clairvoyance and spiritual healing. We have to prove the continuity of life, generation by generation. Do that and the effect must be profound, for once it is realised that the man you kill today you will meet tomorrow wars will be abandoned.

"When I began I joined a Development Circle which sat for nine months before it achieved its first manifestation. The spirits did, however, give occasional directions, such as asking members of the circle to change places so as to get a better 'balance'. One man in the circle began by telling the spirits that he would agree to sit for nine months if that was what they wished. 'I will agree to sit for twelve months if you ask me. But do not ask for nine months and at the end of that time demand another three months. Tell me now, which is it to be: nine months or twelve?' The answer was nine, and nine it was.

"Don't deify spirits. Treat them as intelligent men in another sphere and ask them to give reasons for what they ask. Achieve the utmost cleanliness of mind and body before each seance. Bathe before sitting, and do not smoke or drink for at least three hours beforehand. Above all, seances must be held regularly."

The Society for Psychical Research has published a booklet devoted to hints on sitting with mediums. This disclaims any suggestion that mediums in general, or mediums of any particular type, are necessarily fraudulent. The booklet insists that there are many mediums whose *bona fides* are above suspicion. Although the S.P.R. does not expect all sitters to accept that phenomena observed in the seance room must be of spirit origin, it does suggest that it is best to take these experiences at their face value "at the time of the sitting". This will avoid antagonising the medium and, possibly, his "control", and so invalidating the sitting. Again, many mediums like to create a religious atmosphere in the seance room and so begin each sitting with a prayer. This is in accordance with the Spiritualist's belief that the medium is a link, an intermediary, between this world and the next. "The open flouting of such views," the Society's booklet states, "might well cause offence and lead to null results."

Accordingly, sitters are recommended to adopt a receptive and open-minded attitude while striving to preserve a fair and balanced judgment. It is suggested, however, that if sittings are to have any evidential value precautions should be taken against presenting the medium with a mass of indirect, but nonetheless relevant, information. The very name of the sitter may supply the medium with an important clue which in spite of himself he cannot avoid using. Therefore when arrangements for a sitting are made they should be booked either anonymously or pseudonymously. The sitter ought also to be on his guard not to convey information through his clothing, general appearance, or behaviour, nor supply clues in conversation either before or during the sitting.

Contrariwise, it is wrong, says the S.P.R's booklet, for the sitter to be wilfully unresponsive, argumentative, contradictious, and self-assertive. Persistent questioning of the medium or his control may bewilder and hinder the communications and thus lead to negative results. Again, talkative sitters may over-stimulate the medium's subconscious activity, so that what he gives back is merely an embroidering of what the sitter has told him, while blocking genuine material.

"The sitter's conduct throughout the sitting is highly important," the booklet states. "He may easily spoil and obstruct without intending to do so. It is suggested he should behave as if a Communicator were actually present and striving, *amid much difficulty*, to express what he has prepared to prove his identity. It is by no means essential that one should go with a firm belief in communication from the departed, but it is very desirable to refrain from expressing, or even suggesting, doubt or incredulity during the sitting. The time for criticism and weighing of evidence is when the sitting is reviewed at leisure from notes."

These hints seem to me to be sound, fair, and practical. I should like to think that in my sittings I behaved strictly in accordance with them.

But mediumship is only one aspect of Spiritualism. Nowadays great importance is attached to the ability of those in the spirit world to heal sickness on earth. To this aspect of Spiritualism I now turn.

CHAPTER VIII

DEMONIAC POSSESSION

THE medium was possessed by a demon.

Gripped by a strongly built woman and a young man who would be useful in any Rugger scrum, she drummed with her feet on the floor, screamed at the top of her voice, swore, shrieked gibberish, and wrestled with all her strength to break free.

Mwanga, the spirit of a witch-doctor from the jungles of West Africa, ruled for the time being her mind and body. Because she was in a state of trance, the medium knew nothing of what was going on, but to me, attending for the first time at a casting out of devils, the experience was a terrifying one.

In life, Mwanga must certainly have been a man to be feared. As a diabolic spirit from another world, if that was indeed the explanation of the manifestation I was witnessing, he made my flesh creep.

My surroundings were prosaic enough. The seance was being conducted in the brightly lit basement room of a house in Russell Square, Bloomsbury. The gas-fire gave a cheerful, twentieth-century warmth. The half-dozen people in the room, sitting on every-day Bentwood chairs, who formed the Circle, looked ordinary enough and they were completely unperturbed by what was going on. Four of them I judged to be under thirty years of age. One, a tall, heavily built young woman, acted as secretary and took copious notes. Another was a hospital nurse, although that evening, because she was off-duty, she wore civilian clothes. The medium herself was somewhat older and had been at one time, I was told, a nurse in a mental hospital. In her frenzy she showed that she was a powerful woman. I was afterwards informed that there have been occasions when possessed by demons she has hurled bodily across a table the tough-looking pair whose duty it was to restrain her. When she came to herself she had remembered nothing of these incidents.

There were, however, some unusual pieces of equipment in the room. One was a device for applying ultra-violet rays, as a tonic, to some of the patients who attend the Circle. There was also a Wimshurst machine for generating static electricity by means of friction induced by slowly turning a large wheel. It was a mild shock from this machine which had driven Mwanga from his "host", who was in fact the mildest of small, motherly women, slightly paralysed from a minor stroke. She had wispy hair, and surprised, bespectacled eyes. It was difficult to imagine a more unlikely person for a malevolent savage to haunt. She had come for treatment, so she had told us, because when she went to bed at night "I see some beautiful lights. Lovely they are. And I hear voices." These symptoms had led some Spiritualist friends of hers to suggest that she might be possessed by evil, discarnate spirits.

As it turned out, the lights and voices that had been troubling her were not the results of Mwanga's activity. He had merely been hovering about Russell Square, lying in wait as it were, and when this unoffending little body passed by he had found that her psychical state gave him an easy entry into her "aura", only to be driven out screaming a short time later as the electricity seared his spirit. In pain, for even discarnate spirits, it seems, can be hurt by electricity, he had flown for refuge to the entranced medium, for in that condition part of one's psyche, or personality, vacates the body and thus leaves room for another spirit to take possession. All this is, of course, the Spiritualists' explanation of the phenomena I saw that evening.

A fundamental part of the Spiritualists' creed is that death brings no absolution for wrong-doing on earth. It follows, therefore, that discarnate spirits will be good or evil immediately they have passed over according to what their nature has been on earth. Those who enter the other world begin a spiritual training to fit them for a higher state of existence. Evil spirits resist this training, and they tend to cling to earthly forms. Hence hauntings, poltergeistic manifestations, and demoniacal possession.

It is because of the Spiritualists' conviction that evil spirits exist as well as beneficent ones that many believers, no less than Roman Catholics and many High Anglicans, insist that to dabble in psychic matters can be a highly dangerous practice, especially to those untutored and immature in these subjects. Fooling around with upturned wine-glasses at Christmas parties, table-tilting when imperfectly understood, automatic writing with toy planchettes, and attempts at mediumship, thoughtlessly embarked upon, can have tragic outcomes, so the warning goes, because it is at such times that evil spirits find it easiest to obtain a human lodgment.

Obsession to the point of madness can be the result of all such experiments carelessly begun. Even those with psychic powers they do not so much as suspect may be preyed upon by malignant spirits, for these people also offer an open door-way for the rebellious dead to enter. It is to combat such invasions as these that members of the Marylebone Spiritualist Association have formed an Obsession Circle, adopting the methods of an American investigator, Dr. Carl Wickland. My meeting with Mwanga, the African witch-doctor, took place at a meeting of this Circle.

Dr. Wickland, who is stated in a book he has written, *Thirty Years Among The Dead*, to be a member of the Chicago Medical Society, the Illinois State Medical Society, and the American Association for the Advancement of Science, states that the seriousness of the incidence of mental derangement resulting from ignorant psychic experiment was brought home to him by a number of patients whose seemingly harmless experiences with automatic writing and the Ouija Board, or planchette, had led to such wild insanity that it became necessary to commit them to asylums.

One case he mentions was that of a married woman who, until she took up automatic writing, was "amiable, pious, quiet, and refined". Presently, however, she became boisterous, used obscene language, and imagined that she was an actress with a part to play in a theatre. In the end she became so irresponsible that she had to enter a mental hospital. Another patient who had taken to the Ouija Board believed that God was talking to her and condemning her for sins of which he specifically accused her. She attempted to commit suicide at the instance of this spirit and was taken to an asylum.

Because of these and other instances, Dr. Wickland says, he was himself moved to take up psychic research in the hope of finding a possible explanation for these occurrences. His wife acted as his medium. She appears to have had doubts at first whether it was right to disturb the dead and was reassured by her controls.

"They stated," Dr. Wickland writes, "that there is in reality no death, but a natural transition from the visible to the invisible world, and that advanced spirits are ever striving to communicate with mortals to enlighten them concerning the higher possibilities which await the progressive spirit. But death—the freeing of the spirit from the body—is so simple and natural that a great majority do not, for a longer or shorter period, realise the change, and owing to a lack of education concerning the spiritual side of their natures, they continue to remain in their earthly haunts.

"They maintained that many such spirits were attracted to the magnetic aura of mortals—although the spirit world, as well as the mortal, might be unconscious of the intrusion— and thus, by possessing or obsessing their victims, they ignorantly or maliciously became the cause of untold mischief, often producing invalidism, immorality, crime, and seeming insanity."

In the course of his experiments Dr. Wickland found that the transference of the cause of the psychosis from the patient was facilitated by applying static electricity to the sufferer. This electricity is harmless to the patient, but the possessing spirit cannot long resist it and is dislodged. The medium's

guides then help it to enter this person's aura, when it becomes possible to bring the obsessing entity to a realisation
of its true condition and of its higher possibilities if it will
accept spiritual training on the other side. Dr. Wickland's reply
to the question why those spirits charged with the training
of the newly dead do not take action until this technique has
been adopted is that these earthbound malevolent spirits
cannot be reached by their "tutors" in the other world until
they come in contact with physical conditions, when they are
obliged to realise their true situation and are then started on
the road to improvement. "Unenlightened spirits," he writes,
"often wander aimlessly for many years in the earth sphere,
their lack of knowledge of a higher spirit world, which is
attained only through understanding, keeping them in a dreary
condition of confusion, monotony and suffering; many remain
in the scenes of their earth lives, continuing their former
activities, while others fall into a state of heavy sleep from
which they are with difficulty aroused."

The bulk of Dr. Wickland's book, *Thirty Years Among The
Dead,* is made up of verbatim reports of seances in which he
treated obsessed patients in the manner described. The reports
are dated from 1916 to 1923 and the seances took place
either in Chicago or Los Angeles. The medium was always
Mrs. Wickland. Patients are as a rule identified only by an
initial, and the obsessing spirits range from "Laughing Ella",
"Minnie-on-the-Step" (an orphan), and Ralph Stevenson, a
murderer and suicide, among a large number, to Ella Wheeler
Wilcox and Mary Baker Eddy, the founder of Christian
Science. The detail given in the book has enabled the
Obsession Circle of the M.S.A. to follow his methods exactly
with results that are fairly close to his. This Obsession Circle is
thought to be the only one doing this kind of work in Great
Britain.

On the night when I watched the Circle at work one man
turned the wheel of the Wimshurst electrical machine while
another gently stroked each patient's head from back to
front with one of the terminals from the apparatus. The

second terminal was held by the patient, who sat facing the medium. They were two or three yards apart. The medium sat relaxed, with her hands lightly clasped on her lap. She has the ability of going into trance with unusual ease, and this, I was assured, makes her particularly useful for this type of mediumship. Only a few seconds after the Wimshurst machine began to generate its electricity there was a reaction. The speed of it startled me, for I had expected nothing like it. In that short space the medium was transformed. She raved in a tongue I did not recognise, and had every sign of being consumed by a maniacal fury. I would have thought myself, had I been alone with her, that she was in the throes of a dangerous fit. This, I was informed, was due to the pain inflicted by the static electricity on the obsessing entity. Presently, as the agony abated, the members began to wrestle with Mwanga. Their first act was to persuade him to talk intelligently.

"You must think deep and speak to us in English—you can, you know," said the Circle's secretary, tightly holding one of the medium's arms. There was a pause. The kickings ceased. And then Mwanga began to swear in fluent English.

"Magic, black magic—that's what I practise," he boasted.

"Your magic is powerless against our white magic," the secretary responded confidently.

"I'll put a spell on all you devils," Mwanga shouted. "I'll give that man at the wheel a pill."

"We are not afraid of you," was the retort. "You can't hurt us."

Eventually Mwanga was calmed down and persuaded to go with the spirit guides waiting for him to be cleansed.

"Phew, that was certainly a nasty one," observed the hefty young man who had been helping to hold back the possessed medium. She had now come to herself.

Throughout this seance the patient had sat with an air of meek bewilderment, watching the exorcism. She was advised by the Circle to have spiritual healing in another part of the building, and she was warned that on no account must she practise automatic writing.

"Although you have psychic powers, you must allow no one to persuade you to develop your gifts as a medium," she was instructed. "To do so would be an extremely dangerous act on your part. Otherwise you have nothing to fear. If you come up from the country for another treatment in three months' time that is all that is necessary."

Five patients were seen during the evening. Among them was a young man whose mother's possessive spirit would not allow him to marry. Since her death he had had the home re-decorated in preparation for his wedding, but somehow the sense of his mother's presence had been a barrier to his marriage.

Immediately the wheel of the Wimshurst machine began to turn the medium was in a trance and struggling, though not with the same violence that Mwanga had shown. "Let me get to my boy. I want my boy. My boy needs me. Why won't you let me reach him?" she cried. In this instance it was comparatively easy to calm the possessing spirit and persuade it to accept help on the other side. Once this had been accomplished the medium came out of her trance. She then told the patient, by means of clairvoyance, that he was overconscientious in his work and needed to relax very much more than he was accustomed to do.

Another patient was a middle-aged, talkative Jewish woman, dressed in expensive clothes, whose mind had been seized, it was said, by the spirit of a dead American soldier as she came away from a service she had attended at her synagogue. The symptoms of this spiritual seizure had been a "misty" feeling accompanied by pains in the head. The patient had been to the Circle for help on previous occasions and knew exactly what to do. Once more the wheel began to turn.

In a matter of seconds the medium was again screaming as if in uncontrollable agony. Once more her hands and arms were promptly gripped as she raved and screamed like some-one undergoing torture.

"Why are you doing this to me, you devils?" the medium cried in her trance. "Let me get at her. I *will* get at her. I need somewhere to go. I am tired of wandering."

Once the screams had subsided the members of the Circle questioned the obsessing entity.

"Who are you? Tell us who you are?"

"I won't tell you."

"Then what were you while you were on earth?"

"I was a poor bloody soldier—that's what I was. An American soldier. A Goddamn G.I."

"Then we know you. You have been here before."

"Of course I have been here before. Why do you keep on doing this to me?"

"Because we want to help you."

"I don't want to be helped."

"But you do. That's why you are so tired of wandering."

"I want to do what I bloody well please."

"Oh no you don't. You must learn to go on."

All this time the medium had been fighting to escape. Often she seemed to have difficulty in getting out her words. The voice was her own, not a man's. The spirit was told forcefully that if he wished for peace and happiness he must go with those around him who would help him.

"But they want to put me in hospital and I don't want to go," he protested.

"They want to help you. Have you ever asked them for help?"

"No. I damn well haven't."

"Then say after me, three times, 'Help me.'"

"Help me," the spirit said reluctantly.

"Go on. Three times."

"Help me. Help me."

"Open your eyes. What do you see?"

"Some men in white."

"Go with them."

"Oh, I do feel so tired. I do want to sleep."

The medium quietened and her struggles ceased. Her face

twitched and puckered, like a child's slowly awakening. Presently she opened her eyes.

"Well," said the secretary. "We've got rid of that one."

The patient expressed complete perplexity.

"I'm sure I don't know what it was all about," she said to the Circle at large. "I was walking along quite peacefully, thinking about the service I had been to. It had been such a beautiful one. And then suddenly something came over me. I'm sure I don't understand it."

"Well, you are free now. But it is up to you to stay that way. You must resist these influences all you can. A good tonic will help to build you up."

The next patient was a plump, well-built schoolgirl, with the colour of health upon her cheeks, for whom the diagnosis was that she was not obsessed at all, although many bad spirits were struggling for a place in her aura. This time the medium deliberately did not go into trance because it was feared that her behaviour in that state might be too upsetting for the child. Instead the medium practised clairvoyance and consulted her spirit controls concerning the condition of this girl who had been found at her boarding school to be giving way to certain masochistic tendencies.

When the girl had left the room, the medium told those who had brought her: "They tell me from the other side that this child has had a shock—a sexual shock, you understand—early in life and this has affected her condition. She needs a change of surroundings, something to alter her outlook. Perhaps three treatments with hypnosis would help her."

The last patient that evening was a young woman whose mind had been overthrown by the loss of her sweetheart, an airman, killed in an accident. Until lately she had been in a mental home. This was her third treatment by the Circle. Now she was led in, a pitiful, deranged creature, wearing good clothes and still pretty of face and figure, despite her shrinking, melancholy, vacant expression. Unprotesting, she subjected herself to the technique, and almost at once the Circle were talking through the medium to the spirit of her sweetheart.

"I want to be with X—I want my girlie," he babbled. "Who is this new chap here? I've not seen him before. He doesn't look a bad fellow. I want my girl to be happy. I want to help her."

"Then you must go and be helped yourself."

"But I don't want to be helped."

"When you have learned what you must do, you will understand how to return in the right way so as not to hurt X. As it is, you *are* hurting her."

There followed a long argument. The young man or spirit was stubborn. He protested his affection for the distressed girl, but he was not disposed to accept spiritual training. The session ended unsatisfactorily.

"Well, I can't stay now," the spirit of the airman said through the lips of the medium. "The fellows are going to have a sing-song. I like a laugh. I want X to laugh. I want her to have pretty clothes and look nice when she goes out. Goodbye, everybody."

With his departure X, who had held her head down all this time, not daring to look up, burst into great tearing sobs and a flood of tears.

I have never spent a more harrowing evening.

To balance this picture, I should like to describe the work of Christian psycho-therapy that is being done by the Rev. Edward Barker at Hove. He too believes in the power of the spirit, but it is the spirit of Christ.

Mr. Barker is not a psychiatrist. He does not treat insanity. He is neither a faith-healer nor a proselytiser. But he does pray every day for the improved health of all his patients, and he is a member of a prayer group which offers intercession for the sick. I shall return in Chapter IX to a detailed consideration of the possibility of healing through prayer. Here, however, it is sufficient only to mention that Mr. Barker uses Christianity as a platform from which to bring health to distressed minds.

Mr. Barker is a Methodist minister whose vocal chords had to be removed because of a disability. Now he can speak in no more than a whisper, and this prevents him from preaching. And so he has turned to the healing of those who are spiritually sick. He is striving to fulfil the Biblical injunction: "In my name shall they cast out devils; they shall lay hands on the sick, and they shall recover."

Mr. Barker wears no clerical collar in his consulting room. He works in association with doctors. He trained in psychoanalysis in Harley Street. And he practises, if necessary, light hypnosis. The patients he treats are those suffering from early functional nervous diseases, anxiety states, conversion hysterias, neurasthenia, and compulsive and obsessional neurosis. These states of mind often show up in such forms as insomnia, gastric ulcer, asthma, angina pectoris nervosa, certain skin disorders, bed-wetting, constipation, diarrhoea, menstrual anomalies, or essential hypertension. All this is the medical side of his work. Where he differs from the usual practising psychologist is in his application of Christianity to the healing of distressed minds. He believes he often encounters miracles in his work.

"All healing is a miracle," he has told me, "whether it is done by a surgeon in the operating theatre, the psychologist in his consulting room, or the clergyman at the altar.

"A miracle is not the abrogation of natural law, but the use of other laws we do not fully understand.

"Some time ago I had a patient who said when she first came to me that only a miracle could cure her. She had had shock treatment in a hospital but no therapy, and her symptoms had returned with all their force. On top of this her husband was a compulsive alcoholic. I met her again the other day. 'That miracle I asked for has happened,' she told me. She is completely cured, and is even helping her husband to control his drinking.

"Another patient once asked me what I did when I felt that I needed help myself. I told her that I turned to my hymnbook. She asked to see it, turned over the pages, and asked if she might borrow it. She kept it for six months. When she returned it she said, 'I have read two hymns every morning and another two at night.' By that time her mental disorder had been put right.

"I treat people of all denominations, and to none of them do I directly preach Christianity. That would be, for technical reasons, a mistake. One young patient, a schizoid or split personality, told me at the outset that he was an agnostic. He waited for me to preach religion to him because he wished to tear me to shreds on this issue. But I avoided it. Today he has recovered a good measure of control, has gone to work which he was unable to do before, and has applied for membership of a religious body. Where, however, I find there is a belief in God, I am often able to strengthen that belief and help the patient to a firm hold on life."

There is a strong contrast between the Obsession Circle and Mr. Barker's consulting room; between the screaming, frantic medium, and his gentle, soothing whisper. Yet both are seeking to "cast out devils". Both are exploring tortuous by-paths of the human mind. It may be that a link between the two has been found, unconsciously, by the Rev. Dr. Leslie Weatherhead, of the City Temple, who has said in a recent and most important book, *Psychology, Religion, and Healing*, that he thinks light will be thrown on epilepsy from research into psychic phenomena rather than from psychology. However that may be, I must turn now to a description of what Spiritualism and orthodox Christianity are doing, each in its own sphere, to heal those who are physically sick.

CHAPTER IX

SPIRITUALISTIC HEALERS

LORD DOWDING, the most eminent expounder today of the Spiritualist's creed, has told how he asked a Brains Trust whether statistics have been compiled of the proportion of successes to failures in cures of patients treated by spiritual healing.

"The Question Master," Lord Dowding wrote in his book, *The Dark Star*, "was a prominent Spiritualist who, in accordance with his office, refrained from expressing his own opinion, but I thought that he was a little shaken by the answers received—I know I was. For out of five Brains (all active healing practitioners) who replied, the most pessimistic gave the percentage of successes as 80, and the most optimistic as 95. The only place I happen to know of where strict statistics are kept (including inquiries into after history) is Lourdes, and their percentage of instantaneous cures is about $2\frac{1}{2}$. Of course, the Brains were counting all those cases which yield gradually to continuous treatment, and the Lourdes figure does not include the high proportion of clinical failures whose whole outlook on disease and pain is nevertheless altered by the atmosphere of their pilgrimage, but even so the discrepancy between the figures is enormous. My own little personal experience as a member of a healing circle supported the Lourdes figures, but perhaps we were abnormally inefficient."

I have watched three demonstrations of spiritualistic healing, and my own opinion of its efficacy is similar to Lord Dowding's. My estimate of the number of instantaneous, perfect cures I saw would not differ, I believe, appreciably from his, although the number of people whose condition was helped or whose pain was alleviated must, I agree, be considerably larger. How long that improvement persisted I do not know, but surely it was a wonderful thing that there was any improvement at all, however temporary, in the condition of those patients who received spiritualistic treatment, because many of them had been given up as incurable by their doctors. Mostly they were paralysed, lame, dim-sighted, hard of hearing, arthritic, or rheumatic. They came for spiritualistic treatment as a last hope.

The healers I saw at work would be the last, I am sure, to make exaggerated assertions about their own powers. The Marylebone Spiritualist Association emphasised to me, at the beginning of my inquiries, how important it is that patients should follow up any help they are given with further treatment, otherwise they may revert to their former condition. It is only human nature to flout this requirement. Even so, the most conservative claims made on behalf of Spiritualistic healing by some of its best-known practitioners seem to me to be dazzlingly, unbelievably high.

Mr. Harry Edwards, one of the leading—and most revered —spiritual healers of today has said in his book, *Psychic Healing*, that out of 400 cases a day with which he deals, an average of 80 to 90 per cent report betterment, and of these 30 to 40 per cent are cured. These figures, from one of the leading practitioners, far exceed those of Lourdes, but they are strikingly different from the claims made by the Brains Trust which Lord Dowding questioned. Edwards never states that he can cure or help all or any case that is brought to him. He does not hide his inability to save his best friend when he was dying from meningitis, though he was able, he says, to cure a stranger in a like condition.

At this point I desire to make two things absolutely clear. The first is that psychic, spiritual, spiritistic, and spiritualistic healing—the healing, that is, that is part of the testimony offered in support of the truth of the Spiritualist's hypothesis of life after death—is not faith, divine, or Christian healing, such as I shall describe in later chapters. To the outsider the distinction may be a legalistic quibble, but it is none the less

E

real to a large number of people. The second point concerning which I wish to avoid all misunderstanding is that I have had no means of checking and double checking what I saw and was told at these demonstrations. I am not a medical man. I had no access to the medical histories of these cases. All I aim at doing is to present a faithful report. But in a Court of Law I know that I should make a miserable witness. Much of what I report is merest hearsay, which is inadmissible as legal evidence, even though in our daily lives we commonly accept it when its source appears to us to be trustworthy. This is why the confidence of so many people is pricked to their complete humiliation when they stand in a witness box exposed to legal procedure and the pressures of cross-examination. I am going to tell what I thought I saw and believed I heard, but there is little I can offer by way of corroboration. The reader must decide for himself whether my account has upon it the stamp of truth.

Spiritual healing has been defined by Mr. Harry Edwards as "the removal of disease and other body disharmonies through the employment of spirit forces *via* a human instrument known as a 'healer' or 'healer-medium'." Another well-known writer on psychic matters, Mr. Maurice Barbanell, has explained, in a programme written for one of Mr. Edwards's demonstrations, that the success achieved by this form of healing is based on the "fact" that man is more than a physical body since he has also a soul and a mind. According to Mr. Barbanell, the spiritual healer deals with the causes and not with the effects of diseases. He has a natural gift which he has been at pains to develop. This gift manifests itself in a power streaming through him. Those who benefit from the healer's touch speak of this as a kind of magnetism or heat felt in his finger-tips. It is presumed that human beings have both a physical body and a spirit body (there is here an apparent contradiction of terms). It is this spirit body which survives death. Body and spirit react on each other. Each is profoundly affected by what happens to the other. Spiritual and mental sickness are believed by Spiritualists—and by many others, including orthodox medical men, for that matter—to be the cause of much disease, sickness, and physical degeneration. Similarly broken limbs, burns, and other physical disabilities can lead to spiritual and mental disharmony. Nevertheless, the Spiritualist believes that though the spirit body can be disturbed for a time by physical illness, there is no real and lasting disease in this entity. What is at fault is maladjustment in the physical body. The spiritual healer, it is believed, has the power of transmitting a vivifying force into the suffering patient and so restoring him to health. The spiritual healer is able to achieve "miracles" beyond the capacity of ordinary doctors because he is the channel used by spirits "on the Other Side" who in their new state have progressed far beyond earthly abilities. Nor do they need his actual contact with a sufferer to affect cures, but will, with him as the medium, practise "absent healing" when he is far from the patient but in mental rapport with him. There is, it is held, a "spirit plan" for health. Those "on the Other Side" abhor all suffering on earth. When there is no cure and the sick "pass over" this also is in accordance with spirit purposes; in such cases, however, the spiritual healer believes he can allay suffering and make easier for the dying the passage from this world to the next. Such is the Spiritualist's creed.

Spiritual healing is now systematically organised. Spiritual healers are practising throughout the British Isles. During the last war the Spiritualists in Essex pooled their knowledge, experience, and resources for the common public good of the county, and from this federation there arose the Essex Healers' Association, in which accredited healers combined to provide an Emergency Healing Pool with travelling healers who visit patients in their own homes. They also train candidates in all aspects of healing. This example was copied by Kent, and is now spreading to Surrey, Hampshire, and Yorkshire. The Spiritualist Advisory Healing Council has been formed. This Council is a panel of Spiritualists and healers who advise and give practical help where spiritual healing is needed. The Council aims to inform patients in need of spiritual healing whom they should apply to. It encourages the development of a high standard of healing, for which purpose it holds public meetings, lectures, demonstrations, and study groups.

My first experience of spiritual healing was in September 1951, towards the end of the South Bank Exhibition, when I saw Harry Edwards demonstrate in the Royal Festival Hall. Every seat in the hall had been sold that night. Many who tried to gain admission were turned away. Among the audience were numerous cripples in invalid chairs. Many notables and clergymen were on the platform. Edwards has demonstrated before even bigger crowds in Manchester and Scotland, but this Service of Healing, as it was called, in the heart of London, as a kind of adjunct to the Exhibition, was an outstanding occasion.

Though two hymns and a metric psalm were sung, a passage read from the Bible by a member of the Psychic Youth Club, and a clergyman pronounced the Benediction, there was no suggestion of a revivalist meeting about the service. A religious atmosphere was certainly induced, but nothing resembling hysteria. All the same, as "cure" followed "cure" that night it was possible to sense the emotion generated in the audience.

"We know of no disability that spiritual healing cannot help," it was stated from the platform. "Tuberculosis, diabetes, apoplexy can all be helped in healing circles. Spiritualism goes further than communication with the spirit world. We believe there is a spirit plan and that we can co-operate in its working out. Part of that plan is Spiritualistic Healing."

No one who watched the demonstration that night can have doubted, I am sure, that they saw extraordinary things. Certainly there were no protestations of scepticism either from the audience, the patients, or the clergymen and others on the platform. A paralysed child, carried by its mother on to the stage where Harry Edwards demonstrated in his shirt-sleeves, took its first tottering steps. Crooked spines were straightened. Poker backs were made supple. Limbs that had been locked for years were made flexible once more. And all without the slightest pain to the sufferer. That to my inexperienced lay mind was one of the surprises of the demonstration, for I recalled the agony that normally accompanies the restoration of circulation, the excruciating pain that the rheumatic suffer when "adhesions" are broken down to give mobility once more to an affected joint. None of that was suffered by the men, women, and children whom Harry Edwards treated. With complete assurance his hands passed over spines, legs, arms, shoulders, and hips, pressed this way and that, and then, almost incredibly, the cripples were active again, moving without visible effort or discomfort. It might have been a demonstration of some abnormal power of bone-setting, of osteopathy unusually swift and perfected, were it not for the way in which sight was seemingly restored to the near-blind and hearing to the almost deaf. White programmes were fluttered far back in the hall so that those who had come to the service with their sight wellnigh extinguished could be satisfied how much further they were seeing; and friends called to those who had been treated for deafness so that they could be assured how much better they were hearing.

One man said he had been left paralysed by a stroke. Another asserted he was a sufferer from Parkinson's disease, and that his doctor had said he could do no more for him. Both were appreciably helped back to health, if only momentarily. Edwards asked one of the arthritic cases if she believed she was going to work again? "I hope so—I am trying perseverance," she answered, and at once he commented, "That's courage." He explained that her shoulder was semi-locked. But his hands pressed and fondled at the joint, and presently it was moving freely. Another arthritic case said his wrist had been locked for more than eight years, so that he had not been able to work. For the last two years he had been receiving "absent healing". This man also had his limb restored to activity.

A mother brought a child whose spine was distressingly curved. She said the boy had never walked and that for two years she had been taking him to hospital. Once more Edwards went to work. The crooked spine was straightened

E*

and the "kinked" legs were unlocked. Before long the healer, with the child's hands held in his, was leading him about the platform giving him his first lesson in how to walk.

One more case I must mention. It was that of a young woman who was carried on to the stage in the arms of a man. She was propped in a chair facing the platform, so that Edwards could point out to the audience that hers was what he called a typical instance of poker back. The woman announced that she had contracted disseminated sclerosis. Some of those on the platform, including one or two clergymen and others who said they were medical men, examined the girl and did not dispute the diagnosis. Again Edwards succeeded. Soon he had her touching her toes. "Now," he said, "you can walk lah-di-dah like," and raised a general laugh. The girl took the arm of the young man who had brought her and walked happily off the platform.

For my part I am unable to explain rationalistically all that I saw that night, though I am aware that some psychologists will argue that many such cures are due to the emotionalism and suggestion engendered by such meetings. It is commonly said, too, that once the spotlight of publicity is removed and the patients are no longer the centre of attention the effect wears off, reaction sets in, and their later condition is an aggravation of what it had been previously. This is strenuously denied by those who believe in psychic healing. I am unable to say what the after-history was of those apparent cures, with perhaps one exception.

Three months after that demonstration, in consequence of an article I had written, I received this letter from Mrs. Dorothy Taylor, of 16 Treen Avenue, Barnes, S.W.13: "I was very interested in your article in the *News Chronicle* today [13th December, 1951]. I noticed that you say you were at the Festival Hall when Harry Edwards gave a demonstration. I was one of the cases treated there. I had Disseminated Sclerosis. I am the case you speak of as the poker-back which H. Edwards made to work.

"Well, I thought you would be pleased to know it is still

working, and that I can now walk, and am living an almost normal life as the result.

"I do not know if you know the full details of the case or not, but I must say it was only due to the Absent Healing that I was, and am still getting, from Mr. W. English, of 48 Hesketh Park, Crumlie Road, Belfast, N. Ireland, that I was able to get to the demonstration at all. Mr. English has made a new woman of me.

"The co-operation of these two great Healers has put me on the path to complete recovery. I have just steadily progressed, almost daily, much to the astonishment of most of the neighbours. It is about five months since I started treatment from Mr. English. At the end of two months I had gained two stones in weight. After the demonstration I walked as far round the Exhibition as there was time for.

"I do all my own work, washing and shopping, and am enjoying life to the full."

I admit that letter surprised me. How far it can be accepted as corroboration the reader must decide for himself. To my mind it rings true. And yet, Doubting Thomas that I am, whenever I read similar statements in the psychic press— and they appear there frequently—I confess that my sceptical disposition prevents me from wholly accepting them: I strive to think of some alternative explanation. It is, I realise, because Mrs. Taylor's cure at the hands of a spiritual healer came directly within the orbit of my own experience that I am willing to accept it at its face value. Three months later Mrs. Taylor was still improving and putting on weight. She tells me that before her marriage she was a children's nurse, a hospital nurse for four years, and a dental nurse for two. She admits frankly that before the onset of the sclerosis she had a long history of hysteria. Mrs. Taylor gives equal credit for her improvement to the "absent healing" she received from Mr. English, which taught her to relax and have faith, and to the efforts of Harry Edwards.

There is one more point to be mentioned about the Royal Festival Hall demonstration: Harry Edwards chose all his own patients, pointing to them where they sat and inviting them on to the platform. He did this, it was explained, because it was manifestly impossible for him in the time available to treat all who desired his help. Moreover, he wished, since this was a demonstration, to have as wide a variety as possible of disabilities on which to display his powers. Also, it was said, by taking patients at random he could avoid charges of favouritism and of using fake patients. This last defence, however, cuts, I think, both ways, for by choosing patients it could fairly be argued that he was calling on people whom he had "planted". It would, I am sure, have been more convincing if some other method of selection had been adopted. Even the picking of names out of a hat would have been preferable. But this is the one criticism I would advance.

Who is this man, Harry Edwards, whom so many sick people, not all of them Spiritualists, now idolise? I am told that he is a printer by occupation, though he has now given up this work to devote his whole time to spiritual healing. During the First World War he served in the R.A.M.C., and was posted to India, where ultimately he held the rank of Captain in the Indian Army Reserve. While he was in the East he became intensely interested in Occultism. This turned his attention towards Spiritualism and psychic research. Later he enlisted the friendship of Jack Webber, a well-known medium. This was the friend he was unable to save when sick with meningitis, though he was able, he claims, to allay the pain, violent actions, and convulsions that usually accompany that terrible illness. Edwards has been practising spiritual healing since 1935. He is the founder of the Balham Psychical Research Society, and he now operates from a large house, standing in splendid grounds, at Burrows Lea, near Shere, Surrey. He has two principal assistants, Mr. and Mrs. George Burton, who offered to work for him after seeing one of his demonstrations. He is a man of medium height, stockily built, with silvery hair, and vibrant with energy. One of his most attractive traits is the modesty of his demeanour in public.

Some weeks after the Royal Festival Hall demonstration I watched another healer, Mrs. Nan Mackenzie, at work in the Russell Square headquarters of the Marylebone Spiritualist Association. The room she used, a lecture hall, was crowded with women and children. Some, unable to find chairs, sat outside on the stairs awaiting their turn. Mrs. Mackenzie ranks high among spiritual healers, and is specially beloved because of the way in which she carried on her mission throughout the whole of the blitz on London. Often her healing sessions last from 2 p.m. until 8 p.m., with only a short break for tea —so many are the patients seeking help from her. The receptionist, a motherly little woman, told me that this un-usual "clinic" had been founded by her husband and that she herself had worked there for twenty-four years.

Part of the room was curtained off. Behind these curtains was a medical couch, some chairs, a hand-basin with soap, water, and towels, and a roaring gas-fire, for the day was cold. Mrs. Mackenzie and an assistant both wore white overalls. While she is healing Mrs. Mackenzie is in continual trance, and then her spirit guide, a Red Indian named Running Water, has control of her mind and body. Running Water speaks in a rather stilted voice. He is apt to refer to "the doctor man", and to ask, "That feels good, does it not?" All conversation is with Running Water, and not with Mrs. Mackenzie.

There were no instantaneous cures while I was there, but patients reported progress and brought with them friends and neighbours for help. That indeed is the phrase most often used in connection with spiritual healing. Sufferers do not ask to be cured, nor do healers offer to cure. It is "help" that is sought, and the healers in their turn say, "Let us see if we can help you."

The mother of a little girl who was backward in speaking and given to screaming fits said that since the last treatment the screaming had abated and the child's talking was better. Running Water promptly asked her young patient for a kiss and was given one in the person of Mrs. Nan Mackenzie. Many women came with stiff joints, pains in the back, severe headaches, stomach trouble, blood pressure, and aching ears. Running Water's method was to massage the affected part strongly and to end each movement of her hands with a light snap of her fingers as though she were ridding them of something physically unpleasant. She paid much attention to her patients' spines and the backs of their necks. Running Water believes firmly in the efficacy of herbal prescriptions, of which there was an assortment in the consulting room. I heard her advise two of her patients that if their knees were unduly painful to wrap them up in cabbage leaves before going to bed. "That will draw the uric acid," she said.

When one patient heard that I was there to see how spiritual healing is practised she asked Running Water's permission to tell me of the "spiritual operation" she had had for duodenal ulcer.

"I saw it all in a dream," she told me earnestly. "My little girl, who passed over when she was six years old, was one of the nurses. I saw everything that was done, but I never felt a thing. When I awoke in the morning my arms were locked above my head. I had to ask my husband to unfasten them. I then went to the hospital. An X-ray photograph showed that the ulcer had healed completely. I know it had been removed by the spirit doctors in the other world."

This account encouraged Mrs. Savile, from Mombasa, Kenya, who had been ushered into the consulting room, to tell me her experience. "When I was three years old I displaced a hip," she said. "I remained disabled all my life until I came to Running Water. Doctors and hospitals were unable to do anything for me. Running Water gave me three preparations. Then I got on to that couch, and she put the hip back into place without any trouble. That was in 1949. My age now is fifty-two. I returned to Africa, completely well for the first time in my life. Since then worry and the climate of Mombasa have upset me. I have developed high blood pressure and other symptoms. So I have made another journey from Africa to consult Running Water. Already my general health is tremendously improved. I want everyone to know the benefit I have had."

By this time one pressing question was obtruding itself upon my mind: Can spiritual healing, which asserts it can give "help" in so many instances pronounced by doctors to be incurable, benefit cancer patients in any way? The answer that the Spiritualists give is: Yes—if it is part of the "Spirit plan" that the sufferer should be helped, and even if a cure is not possible the spirits will still act through the mediumship of a psychic healer to alleviate pain and ease the passing. This answer of the Spiritualists tallies very closely, as we shall see, with that of certain Christian healers when faced by the same challenge to cure cancer. The Christian healer confidently expects faith and prayer to work a miracle, but if the divine plan makes recovery impossible the sufferer will still be helped, by his trust in the Almighty, to "die well". The difference between the psychic healer and the faith healer is this: The psychic healer attributes any cure at his hands to the intervention of his "spirit guides" in the next world, whereas the faith healer believes that he is the channel through which Christ is able still to exercise the ministry of healing He practised while on earth.

Harry Edwards, in his book on *Psychic Healing*, gives some instances of cancers he asserts he has cured by spiritualistic methods. He says that some cancers can be dispersed by his guides either through the bowels or by means of excessive perspiration. Nor is he by any means the only practising Spiritualist to believe that Spiritualism can cure cancer as well as the other diseases mentioned earlier in this chapter. I therefore determined to see Harry Edwards following his mission of healing not at a distance, as a member of an audience in the body of a large hall, but at close quarters. Accordingly I went down on a day at random to Burrows Lea, Shere, where, deep in the Surrey countryside, he sees his patients personally on three afternoons a week. The only warning I gave him was to telephone him that morning to ask if it was convenient for me to come. Without hesitation he invited me to his home and told me that at Dorking railway station I should find a private motor-coach he uses to convey his patients out to Burrows Lea, about six miles away.

During the journey to Dorking I noticed sick and crippled people joining the train. To my mind it was utterly improbable that a special gathering of fake patients was being assembled for my benefit, and this removed the shadowy doubt that had been in my mind, as I have already mentioned, at the Royal Festival Hall, when only those people had been invited on to the platform whom Edwards had himself chosen.

The patients treated at Burrows Lea are but a few of the hundreds of sick people to whom Harry Edwards daily gives "absent healing". The demand to see him is so prodigious that he has a waiting list extending months ahead. Patients travel long distances to entreat his help.

The Sanctuary, as he calls it, in which Edwards tries to succour the sick and the disabled is a large, light, airy, oak-panelled room, lavishly decorated with exquisite flowers. Those who waited for treatment faced a massive wooden table. On this were placed vases of magnificent white and bronze chrysanthemums, a pair of silver candlesticks, and a symbol, fashioned out of transparent plastic, of a cross inside a circle. The atmosphere in the Sanctuary, in contrast to that at the Royal Festival Hall demonstration, was almost clinical, and was certainly aseptic, though I have never known a hospital where the operating theatre was embowered with flowers, and the waiting patients, instead of student doctors, watched the treatments.

One by one the patients moved up the room to where, at right angles to them, Mr. Edwards sat with his two helpers, Mr. and Mrs. George Burton, who are both considerably younger than he is. I sat at Edwards's side all afternoon, as near to him as I could possibly be. Wearing a white coat, a shirt open at the neck, and a pair of grey flannel trousers, he saw about twenty-five sufferers that afternoon. No fees were asked for, but at the door there was a plate for freewill offerings, but how much was placed in it I do not know.

Unlike Mrs. Mackenzie, Mr. Edwards does not go into a trance while healing. He believes he is a channel used by a group of spirit healers at whose head are Louis Pasteur and

Lord Lister. These spirit guides pour through his hands a healing power able to remove the disharmonies of which the patient's illness is a symptom.

He begins his sessions with a silent prayer. He next attunes himself to his spirit guides, and then, by taking hold of the hands of the patient sitting facing him in a chair, he tries to blend his personality with that of the sick person. A quick movement of his hands over the patient's body tells him where the trouble is located—chest, spine, heart, head, stomach, or limbs.

I watched him place his fingers on either side of the nose of a man suffering from sinus trouble. Within a few seconds the blocked passages were cleared by no method visible to me —certainly by no kind of massage. The patient said he had been medically operated on a number of times for his complaint. The last operation had taken place about six months earlier. His condition was as chronic as it had ever been. Within a few days he was emigrating to Rhodesia and so he had come for help as a last resource. Edwards had told him his sinus passages were completely blocked. He ordered the patient, a Welshman, to breathe in. "Breath deeper," he said. "Shut your mouth. Now the left nostril. Now the right. Now both together. There now," he ended triumphantly.

"Oh, lovely," said the patient. "It has never been like that. But will it keep that way?"

"There is no reason why it shouldn't. Use an inhaler. You help us, and we will help you."

Similarly, I watched him stroke, with a few quick movements, the knees of a white-haired man suffering from osteo-arthritis. "You are all right now," Edwards told the patient to the man's obvious disbelief. But he got up, found he could walk freely and painlessly, and then threw away his stick as a gesture of confidence.

Mr. Edwards made me feel how one girl's spine was out of place and how another was "spastic"—hard and contracted. Within no more than seconds under his hands they returned to normal. Again I emphasise that I have no medical experience of any kind. I would not dream for an instant of diagnosing what was wrong with those people nor hazard a guess at what had been done for them. I do not know how long their improvement continued. But I did feel for myself the malformations of their spines. I was invited to place my hand on the breast of a middle-aged woman who was greatly alarmed because of a mysterious lump she had lately discovered. Edwards asked her if she had consulted a doctor, and she replied she had not because she was too afraid of what she might be told. He advised her to seek medical assistance, but he did not turn her away. He kept his hands upon her breast and presently he announced that the lump was considerably diminished. I was asked to feel it for a second time. I am too unversed in these matters to say by how much, if at all, that lump had abated.

And so it went on all afternoon. The healer was modest. He made no confident promises. "Let us see what we can do," was all he offered, and often he told his patients that cures would take time. One particularly distressing case was that of a youth whose arms and legs were horribly malformed, so that all the movement he was capable of was a kind of hesitant shambling when supported by his father. Edwards promised no speedy cure. "Keep writing to me and see me again in three months' time," he said.

Mostly he seemed to pour his own abounding health into the suffering person whose hands he held. I watched him pull a woman together who was in an advanced state of nervous collapse. She had dropped on to the chair in front of Edwards as lifelessly as a sack of potatoes. She was without "backbone", drooping, weak, tremulous, and about to dissolve into tears. Edwards appeared to take her into his hands, remould her, and give her back her mettle. The tears went, and smiles broke upon her face. Once more vigour came back into her frame. I cannot say how long that change was to last, but when she passed through the doorway on her way home she was a woman transformed.

When the last patient had been seen, we went into the sitting-room of the house for a cup of tea so that I could ask him some questions that had been puzzling me. He explained that he no longer uses the trance technique, which he formerly adopted, because he found it made strangers uneasy. It has become unnecessary for him to go into trance because of the pitch which his mediumship has now reached.

Mr. Edwards told me that he receives some 1,500 letters a day from people asking him for help. He has lately treated, he says, his *millionth* patient. Each letter is annotated by his staff and passed to him. At night, in the quiet of his room, he offers prayers for these sufferers as part of his method of "absent healing". These prayers, however, are not addressed to God, Jesus Christ, or the communion of saints, but to his healing guides in the spirit world. It is important to remember this because it differentiates Mr. Edwards's work from that of the Christian faith healers which I shall describe in a later chapter. Mr. Edwards names each patient and the patient's address to the spirit guides—Lord Lister, Pasteur, and the rest. The healer formulates in his mind a picture of each sufferer's complaint and asks the spirit guides to remove the "disharmonies" that are responsible for it. For these spirit guides neither time nor distance exists, say the Spiritualists, and from this it follows that Harry Edwards, communing in the Sanctuary of his Surrey country home, can obtain spiritual aid for patients anywhere in the world. Nor is it necessary, according to the Spiritualists' creed, that the sick should themselves write to a healer. It is sufficient if a friend does so on their behalf so long as adequate details of the patient's condition are provided. Mr. Edwards argues that this demolishes the common argument that spirit healing is a psychological reaction. This form of absent healing can be administered to ailing infants, the mad, and those who strenuously oppose the tenets of Spiritualism. Even without a patient's knowledge or consent absent healing can, it is asserted, be effectively administered.

One of Mr. Edwards's most important dogmas is this: "Success with absent healing is almost entirely dependent upon the healer's ability to 'tune-in' with his spirit doctors,

plus the second essential of his utmost confidence in the power
of the spirit healing guides to overcome any complaint. The
healer must never, within his own mind, limit the possibilities
of a restoration." We shall see later that the Christian
therapists say exactly the same thing when acting as channels
for divine healing.

Edwards says that in his experience spirit influences
brought into play through absent healing have cured drink
and drug addicts. Married couples who have separated
have been brought together again. Epilepsy and other
mental and nervous diseases have been cured. The mad
have been restored to sanity. Heart and blood disorders have
been put right. Finally, skin and stomach complaints have
been healed.

Mr. Edwards purposely practises his absent healing late
at night, for he judges that this is the time when the sufferers
for whom he seeks aid will be asleep or at least resting. He
believes that the spirit guides are best able to accomplish
their work when the patients are completely relaxed. States
of mental stress and the anxious watching for signs of improvement are barriers to the healing efforts of the spirits.

I was shown the thick files in which Mr. Edwards keeps
his "case-histories". Taken at their face value they make a
most impressive battery. I thumbed through them at random,
and was astonished by the variety of sickness—often sup-
posedly incurable sickness—and the width of the geographical
boundaries they embraced. Here I must add that I have
investigated none of the reputed cures, for I am a layman
and consequently am debarred from access to the medical
records of these patients. I can merely record that these files,
taken by themselves, are surprisingly voluminous.

Presently one of Mr. Edwards's helpers interrupted our discussion. She said that a family had that moment arrived by
car from Cornwall and must return the same night. Would Mr.
Edwards see them? He had just poured himself another cup of
tea. Uncomplainingly, he placed the saucer on top of the cup
to keep the tea hot and went out into his room of healing.

CHAPTER X

DIVINE FAITH AND CHRISTIAN HEALING

THE surgeon leaves the operating theatre and comes to deliver his verdict of life or death.

"I have done all I can," he says. "To do more is beyond my powers. You must pray now for a miracle."

So the distressed go away. They do pray and miracles do happen. An increasing number of doctors are saying so.

Until a short time ago I had never questioned the inference that anyone known to be suffering from cancer was under sentence of death, except in those instances of early diagnosis when surgery and deep X-rays can do their curative work. But lately I have heard so much of the healing power of prayer that now my attitude is changing.

Dr. T. Howard Somervell, the mountaineer and a Fellow of the Royal College of Surgeons, has told in his autobiography, *After Everest,* of a patient in Southern India who had a cancer of the cheek that was so advanced he declined to operate. The man went home and persuaded members of his church to pray for him frequently. "Months later," says Dr. Somervell, "I went to the branch hospital near his place of abode, and a stalwart, healthy man with a healed scar on his cheek came to see me. The cancer, incurable by any method known to medical science, except radium and X-rays, had completely disappeared.

"I confess that in my weakness of faith I was amazed, but of the original diagnosis there can be no doubt. If we in Neyyoor, where we see five or six hundred cases of cancer of the mouth every year, cannot diagnose a case of it, who can? Explain these cases how you like, by the power of the mind over the body, or by the intervention of God—the fact remains that their faith had been exercised in a way of which in our materialistic England we have no experience."

Actually we in England have an increasing testimony of similar experiences, though—and here is the essential weakness, the fatal flaw, you may think—there is usually very little sound, corroborative evidence to support them. Many statements are made about "miracle" cures, but usually they are woefully vague about names, dates, and addresses. We wish to know who were the doctors who attended these patients and expect to read their sworn accounts of what happened. But all this is withheld from us. When we come to reflect about this we see it is natural. It is a tradition of western medicine that the doctor should work in strictest privacy. Even the text-books of medicine preserve the anonymity of patients. Case-histories are not submitted on oath, and should any investigator wish to check them individually he will find it virtually impossible to do so. The text-books, however, are written for an expert audience, who will detect absurdities, exaggerations, and errors of technique. The professional reputation of the authors is a sufficient guarantee of the integrity of their work, and so it is accepted. Just so does the layman accept Dr. Somervell's account of the Indian who was healed by prayer of cancer, even though it is manifestly impossible for the sceptic to go to Neyyoor and verify it for himself.

Inquirers of the most various kinds have all found it well-nigh impossible to obtain acceptable corroboration when investigating the supposed cures of unorthodox healers. Canon L. W. Grensted in his Bampton Lectures, *Psychology and God*, given before the University of Oxford in 1930, declared that the Committee on Spiritual Healing appointed by the Archbishops of the Church of England had tried to extract such evidence after two faith-healing missions had been loudly acclaimed as successful. "In one case," Canon Grensted wrote, "there was a long printed list of specific healings, several of these being healings of physical disorder of the most explicit character. Yet letters sent to every doctor and to every clergyman in the districts concerned failed to produce any information as to the real nature of these more definitely organic cases.

It should be added that there was plenty of evidence of the cure of 'functional' disorders, and, which is the greatest achievement of these missions, of spiritual conquest and of peace of mind brought even to those who were not healed. In such disorders as consumption this alone is no mean advance towards health." Canon Grensted asserted that the same was true of those who had essayed a similar task in connection with Christian Science.

Occasionally, however, in the midst of the general vagueness, some accounts do emerge that appear to be better authenticated than the others. One of these is the testimony of Dr. Cyril Woodard, who has been styled "the athlete's specialist". Dr. Woodard, whose medical qualifications are high, served as a naval surgeon during the war in the Mediterranean. During his service he had a number of experiences of the recovery of patients that were outside what medical practice would have expected. But it was the "raising from the dead", as he believes, of his own small son that has changed Dr. Woodard's entire conception of faith-healing possibilities. In his absence the boy was admitted to hospital suffering from one of the worst forms of meningitis. When the father hurried to the ward and saw the child he believed he had arrived too late. But he laid his hands upon the boy and prayed for him. The child was immediately restored and is now a healthy, active lad at a public school. Since then Dr. Woodard has been healing, as he says, "in the name of Christ". He is an active member of the Church of England. Lately he has thrown up his Harley Street practice to join the Rev. John Maillard at Milton Abbey, Dorset, where, with other helpers, they are practising Christian therapy among the chronically sick.

The Rev. W. E. Sangster, of Central Hall, Westminster, who is one of the most influential of present-day Methodist ministers, has told me how one of his women workers had a breast removed because it was cancerous. Two years later the same symptoms appeared in the other breast, and she was told she must have it removed because it was malignant. Before she agreed to go into hospital her father asked her if her faith was strong enough to believe that prayer could cure her. That night she held a vigil, during which she prayed for her faith to be strengthened. About 3 a.m. the feeling came to her that the faith she was praying for would be granted to her.

The next evening she went with her father to a Fellowship meeting. Half-way through the service she touched her breast and found that she could not feel the lump which she knew to be there. She and her father hurried home. She examined her breast and found that the lump had gone. She has had no recurrence of the trouble. That woman is now the devoted leader of a prayer circle.

Dr. Sangster has also told me of a Methodist missionary who returned from Africa so ill with tuberculosis that no hospital would admit him, for they felt they would be wasting a bed in which another life might be saved. So an empty manse was found for him in the West Country where he might die in comfort. The manse would not be needed until the following September. But the Prayer Circle at Central Hall, Westminster, interceded for him. September came and he was still alive. Three years later he was not only alive but intensely active. It is his ambition to preach one day at Central Hall.

The Rev. Leslie Weatherhead, of the City Temple, has described in his book, *Psychology, Religion, and Healing,* how Andrew Caird, a surgeon at Carlisle, operated on a woman and found cancer of the stomach too far advanced for further surgical treatment.

"He removed a small piece of tissue and sent it for pathological examination," Mr. Weatherhead writes. "Cancer was confirmed. The woman had been stitched up and sent home to die. Caird declared that she could not live for more than a fortnight. Her friends, however, met together regularly to pray for her recovery. Seven years later she was married and is still completely well (1950). Caird himself said that the only explanation he could give was that she was healed in answer to prayer."

Then there is the case of Matthew Peiris, a motor engineer in Ceylon, who has been healed of a tumour in the brain, says a recent *Newsletter* of the London Healing Mission, a Church of England organisation, through the intercession and ministry of the Church. The Mission has opened an ordination fund for Peiris, who is married and has two small children, to support him and his family while he undergoes theological training, since in gratitude for his recovery he desires to be ordained.

Dr. Rebecca Beard, who practised medicine in America for twenty years until she gave it up in favour of spiritual healing, has told how Alice Newton, of Leavenworth, Kansas, was healed of cancer by the power of her faith. Her abdomen, says Dr. Beard, was terribly swollen, her body emaciated, and her condition feeble. But she asked the doctor: "Do you think I can be healed with prayer and nothing else?"

Dr. Beard said she did so believe.

"All right," Mrs. Newton replied. "I'll do it for you and for my husband. I have absolute faith now that our prayer will be answered and the Lord will heal me."

Mrs. Newton went home. She did simple things about the house, rested, walked in the open air, read her Bible, sang hymns, and prayed. Finally one night it happened. She dreamed of the Crucifixion and awoke at 3 a.m. to find that her abdomen was flat.

"Where did thirty-eight and a half pounds of actual weight go in three hours?" Dr. Beard asks. "That was the miracle. I examined her and found every organ fresh and virginal as though she had never been ill. She lives today. During the past twelve years the Leavenworth newspaper and the *Kansas City Star* have mentioned this recovery each January on the anniversary of Alice's healing."

When I read this in Dr. Beard's book, *Everyman's Search,* I cabled to the Editor of the *Kansas City Star* and asked him to confirm this healing of Mrs. Alice Newton. I received no answer, although a reply was prepaid. That silence proves nothing, but it does show, I suggest, how difficult it is to obtain outside verification.

Dr. Beard says that her own medical practice was cut short when her medical colleagues told her that she must put her affairs in order because she could not live through another heart attack. With the shock of that announcement there came what she calls a wonderful revelation, a great spiritual illumination. "I knew then that I was healed," she writes, "and I knew that the rest of my life would be given to helping others find that healing." She became acquainted with Mrs. Agnes Sanford and some more American spiritual healers, and in the spring of 1947 she and her husband gave up their home and went to Merrybrook to begin their work in spiritual therapy. She has already achieved an international reputation.

One woman who has lately aroused widespread interest because of the ministry of healing she has been undertaking within the framework of orthodox Christianity is Mrs. Elsie Salmon of South Africa, where her home has been for the last twenty years. She is the wife of a Methodist minister in Pretoria and the mother of three sons. The Rev. Dr. W. E. Sangster, of Central Hall, Westminster, remembers her thirty years ago as a girl from the West Country who was already winning a reputation as a vocalist. She was engaged to one of his college friends, and when duty took him to South Africa she went out there, was married, and so took on the obligations of a minister's wife.

Suddenly, about nine years ago, Elsie Salmon stumbled on the fact that she was a channel of divine healing. Christ was using her, or so she came to believe, to heal the sick when she touched them with her hands. Since those early days she has treated 20,000 white and coloured people, as well as Jews, Chinese, Indians, and Japanese, Christians and unbelievers alike. She has travelled tirelessly about South Africa performing this work. On one healing mission that lasted three weeks she covered 2,875 miles and "laid hands" on nearly 3,000 people. Arthritis, tuberculosis, growths, asthma, and paralysis are among the morbid conditions which she has successfully healed, even when medical men had pronounced the sufferers to be incurable.

"In all the 20,000 cases treated the power has never failed to come through," Mrs. Salmon has written in a little book,

He Heals Today, in which she has recounted the story of her healing ministry. By "power" she means a healing force emanating from her hands. This force manifests itself as heat which penetrates deeply through the patient's body and may even burn the skin. This is how she describes it:

"The power seems to be strongest after regular intervals of time, and I know that, given the right conditions, I can expect at least some instantaneous (perfect) healings at those times when the power seems to be strongest."

This force, as it flows through her hands, varies with the patient's disease. Sometimes it is like an electric current, she says, sometimes like a cool shower, or even like strong sunlight.

"Some patients feel no power at all, but sense a wonderful presence and peace," she continues. "I often feel a hand on my shoulder and I know that He is there."

Among the cures that Mrs. Salmon describes are some that read, by the rational standards we normally apply, like the wildest fiction. The story of three-year-old Mildred is one such instance. This child was born without a left hand, so that her arm ended in a point no bigger than an index finger well above the wrist. Mildred's mother approached Mrs. Salmon, showed her the deformed arm, and asked her if she could help. She countered by enquiring whether the mother believed that Christ could create a hand and the reply was that she did so believe.

"You are someone after my own heart," Mrs. Salmon cried. "I, too, believe we dare not limit the power of God."

Within a month of the mother's protestation of faith, the point at the end of Mildred's deformed arm had doubled in size and was quite plump. Another month passed, and then it was noticed that the arm was lengthening and that the circulation was better.

"People who knew the child were watching developments with keen interest and faith," Mrs. Salmon says. "The following month there was a formation which looked like a thumb and which, at the time, we thought was a thumb." Three months later, however, it was found that this formation was not a thumb at all, but a hand at the end of the child's arm. This was seen gradually to unfold like a flower. Bones formed and wrist bracelets developed. Then four clenched fingers appeared, followed by signs of fingernails. This was after two years' "treatment" by faith and prayer.

"The mother and I often wonder how the final unfolding of the fingers will take place, but one thing is certain—there is absolutely no doubt in the minds of the hundreds of people who have been following developments that a perfect hand is forming and by the time she needs it it will be there," so Mrs. Salmon concludes her account of the hand that grew. It is backed by a doctor's certificate, but, in deference to medical etiquette, the name and address of the doctor are suppressed. Nor is the identity disclosed of Mildred and her parents. When Mrs. Salmon's book was published, however, I cabled to Cape Town and instructed one of the most reputable newspapermen there to carry out an independent inquiry concerning the healing of this deformed child before publishing a review of *He Heals Today*. Because of the distance between Cape Town and Pretoria, Mrs. Salmon's residence, there was a little delay, but eventually the story was confirmed and the information was given that the little girl had continued to progress. I am forced, therefore, to accept the authenticity of this "miracle". Moreover, Mrs. Salmon's work is backed by Mr. Gordon Mears, a former Cabinet Minister in the South African Government, by Mr. Arthur S. Wood, a solicitor in Cape Town, and by at least five Methodist ministers.

Mrs. Salmon's book is a short one, but it relates many instances of how, by faith, prayer, and the laying of her hands upon sufferers, she has enabled cripples to lay aside their crutches, the bedridden to walk, pain to disappear, and ulcers to be healed. Addison's disease, phlebitis, sinus, enteritis, gallstones, palsy, leukaemia, barrenness—all these have yielded to her "power". The one terrible scourge she does not mention is leprosy. I have noticed this same omission in the accounts of healing written by many faith, divine, Christian, and Spiritualist healers, and because of the emphasis which the Bible places upon the healing of lepers, and the amount of work done by missionaries to help these stricken people, I admit I find this passing over of leprosy to be curious. I am sure that none of these healers would say that leprosy is beyond the scope of their power, but I am left wondering why it is they have not taken it into this field.

The amount of medical evidence which Mrs. Salmon offers is restricted. She emphasises that she is no diagnostician and that she has only a limited knowledge of pathology and anatomy. What patients tell her as purporting to come from their doctors after medical examination she accepts. Because of this dearth of medical testimony, are we to dismiss her account? It is a critical question, and every reader will answer it for himself. Personally I am forced to believe that at the services she conducts she does heal many extremely ill people. These cures may be due, as she believes, to a divine agency. They may be the result, as some are sure to argue, of the patient's faith, or, what I find more plausible, remembering the children and the non-Christians she has helped, to the healer's own faith. It may even be, to put the rationalist's inevitable argument, that the hysteria associated with revivalism—and Mrs. Salmon is a revivalist—is responsible. But what the explanation is I confess I do not know.

I have no wish to appear either sceptical or credulous. I should like to know what to believe. If one dismisses Mrs. Salmon's own explanation as too fantastic for a scientific age to accept, then I know of no theory to cover all the facts she gives, if facts they are and not the products of an extraordinary instance of mass deception or mass hallucination.

Divine healing is to Mrs. Salmon a part of evangelism, of her mission of "winning souls for Christ". She insists that before a healing service the sufferer must first prepare himself spiritually. The patient then attends a mission service, during which he receives at the communion rails the ceremony of the laying on of hands.

"Many seek Christ for the first time in a healing mission," Mrs. Salmon writes. "Where the ground has been well prepared beforehand by much prayer, there the blessings are manifold. I have known a minister and his wife to prepare a congregation by five weeks of prayer and meditation in the church where the mission was to be held. It is not surprising that an 'atmosphere' is created and great blessings follow."

For the treatment itself she asks her patients to relax and so induce a receptive mood. She prays both before and after the laying on of hands. Silence during this ceremony she finds essential.

She tells how once, when she touched a patient, "I felt as though my hands had been severed at the wrists, and as if my life's blood was pouring out in a steady stream." Nor has she actually to touch a sufferer for a cure to be effected. She can heal the absent by praying for them, and has a special prayer list on which are the names of patients who cannot come personally for various reasons. Every morning at seven o'clock thousands of intercessors all over South Africa link up in prayer on behalf of the 4,000 sufferers who have sought her aid. The parallel between her methods and those of the Spiritualist healers is strikingly close, except in the important matter of the agent to whom the cure is attributed.

Mrs. Salmon is not working alone as a divine healer of an orthodox Christian denomination. There are others like her both in America and this country. One well-known American name is that of the Rev. Roland Brown. I have already mentioned Dr. Rebecca Beard. Another revered American healer is Ruth Robison, who has said that although she does not presume to know when it is time for any of her patients to die, she does know that none of them need die sick; all, through faith, can die well. Perhaps the best loved of all this group is Mrs. Agnes Sanford. She is the daughter of a Presbyterian missionary in China and is now the wife of an Episcopalian rector. Her ability to heal is similar to that of Mrs. Salmon, although her book, *The Healing Light,* gives no instance so striking as that of the hand which grew. Even so, she too asserts she has known prayer to heal cancers.

Once when she laid her hands on a little girl who had been

immobilised for five months after being stricken with infantile paralysis the child cried out because of the heat that was coming through Mrs. Sanford's hands. Within a fortnight the girl was walking.

Mrs. Sanford contends that forgiveness and healing are one. This has become one of the fundamental principles of those who practise divine healing. Sometimes the sick can heal themselves by their own power of faith, but the most powerful healing method of all, so Mrs. Sanford believes, comes from the faith of someone else acting "as a receiving and transmitting centre for the life of God". And she lays down, as a law of prayer, that those who pray must believe that they are receiving whatever blessing they are praying for. "If we are going to pray effectively," she says, "we must believe that the thing for which we pray is at that moment being accomplished." The outline of her method is this:

Choose the same time and the same place every day, make yourself comfortable and relax.

Remind yourself of the reality of a life outside yourself.

Ask for life to come in and increase the life in your body.

Make a picture on your mind of your body well.

In this way she was able to heal herself when suffering from cysts and a collapsed organ. Her own prayers, it is true, proved insufficient, but before consenting to a surgical operation she called on the help of intercessors. "With this additional help," she writes, "I began to perceive as I prayed for healing a drawing-up sensation and a distinct vibration and warmth in the lower abdomen. Moreover my increased vigour and relief from pain indicated that a process of rebuilding was taking place." When she finally went back to her doctor he rebuked her. He had asked her to attend twice a week for treatment, but she had not been to see him for a year. On examining her, however, he declared she was perfectly healed. Nevertheless she does not spurn medical aid. In sickness she looks upon the doctor as her best friend and adviser.

Mrs. Sanford tells how she was able to help one woman who was in hospital with a severe abdominal swelling. The growth was too advanced to be removed surgically, and the patient's heart was weak, her blood count bad, and there was sugar in her blood. The doctors believed that an operation must end fatally. But Mrs. Sanford laid her hands on the sufferer and prayed in response to an appeal from the dying woman. "I believe you will get well, and we will leave the method to God," she said. Three months later the patient's heart and circulation were normal. The growth, however, was larger than ever. The patient took this as a sign that God was waiting for the doctors to help Him. She insisted on an operation. It was naturally a severe one and occupied three hours. She was prayed for continually. Two days later she was sitting up in bed polishing her finger-nails. She made a perfect recovery.

Mrs. Sanford recounts what she did when she found a neighbour named Williams unconscious from a heart attack. "I sat down on the arm of his chair and placed my hands above and below the heart. It was beating precisely as the kettle-drum beats in Strauss's *Death and Transfiguration*—insistently, irregularly, terrifyingly. (I found out later that the heart had swollen until it filled almost the whole chest and that every valve had burst and was leaking like a sieve.) . . .

"As soon as my hands were firmly upon his heart, I felt quiet, serene, in control. Forgetting the man's heart, I fixed my mind upon the presence of Our Lord and invited him to enter and use me. Then, Mr. Williams being quite unconscious, I talked informally to the heart, assuring it quietly that the power of God was at this moment re-creating it and that it need labour no longer. Finally, I pictured the heart perfect, blessing it in the name of the Lord and giving thanks that it was being re-created in perfection. Soon I could feel the heart-beats becoming more quiet and regular. . . . By the time the doctor came, the patient had walked upstairs and gone comfortably to bed." Two days later Mr. Williams's heart was reported to be normal in size once more. Mrs. Sanford's behaviour on that occasion must have called for unusual courage—and supreme faith.

In contrast to the way in which she, Dr. Beard, and Ruth Robison go about their healing are the methods employed by another American faith healer, Mr. Oral Roberts, of Healing Waters, Tulsa, Oklahoma. I intend no denigration of Mr. Roberts when I call him the apotheosis of Revivalism. I believe it is a term he would regard as a compliment. Certainly he uses every device at his disposal to bring healing through faith to the people of the U.S.A. He pitches his huge Gospel Tent in towns throughout the States and with the co-operation of numerous clergymen preaches his creed to crowds thousands strong at a time. A magazine he publishes, *Healing Waters*, is said to have a circulation of 115,000 copies a month. It is lavishly illustrated with photographs of men, women, and children who testify that they have been healed at his services. "The blind see again," say the captions. "The stutterer talks again. The tubercular breathes again. The deaf hear again." And always in the pictures, in addition to the sufferer and Mr. Roberts, there is a microphone. Every Sunday his religious broadcasts are radiated by more than a hundred stations in thirty-six states. His text is from James: "The prayer of faith shall save the sick." One notable feature concerning the accounts of Oral Roberts's cures is that they are accompanied by full details of names and addresses, and usually by photographs. Many of the cures are of afflictions that might well spring from hysteria—speech defects, imperfect sight and hearing, hay fever, epilepsy, drug-taking, and mental disorders. Cancer and tuberculosis do, however, figure prominently. One woman writes that her son-in-law, a soldier, has been saved from the "tobacco-habit". Another message is from a man aged seventy who says he had been sick for more than a year and had been given up to die. "I had heart trouble, asthma, rheumatism, and was blind in one eye," he writes. But now God has healed him through one of Roberts's broadcasts, and the sufferer adds: "I wasn't able to go out of the house, but now I am feeling fine and can eat and sleep, get up early and stay up late. May God bless you and the work you are doing." The joy of the "saved" animates almost every one of the testimonies.

One writer says that Roberts's face "shines" as he preaches in the Gospel Tent. When he seizes the microphone and jumps from the platform the crowd rise to him "like covies of flushed quail" and run to meet him. A long line forms on his left. He lays his hands on the head of each sufferer and reminds Jesus of his promise to heal the sick. It may take two hours for the line to file past him. Cripples are seen to straighten up and walk naturally. Many appear to be miraculously helped. Some declare they have been converted merely by watching the scene.

Roberts began his healing ministry one Sunday in May 1947 in the Educational Building, in Enid, Oklahoma. "When I returned to Enid forty-two months later," he writes, "after having conducted healing campaigns from coast to coast and border to border of this nation before more than three million people face to face and having won over 100,000 souls to Christ and ministered healing to multitudes, the Enid people insisted that we secure the Convention Hall which had a much larger seating capacity than the Educational Building I had used for my first healing service.

"This time 4,000 people jammed into Convention Hall, breaking an all-time attendance record for any gathering in the city of Enid, to hear the Word of God. Several hundreds were turned away at the doors as Enid opened its heart to me. We had 1,200 for my first service; the next one, forty-two months later, we had 4,000.

"I shall always be glad I proved the Lord's call to me. It had enabled me to have a steady, continuous faith that God is with me. One cannot doubt something he knows is true. I know I am called of God to minister God's healing to my generation. For this cause I came into the world."

We are too shy in this country to follow Mr. Oral Roberts's methods. Our churches prefer to do their healing surreptitiously, almost in secret. There is a lively fear that if it became widely known it might attract the wrong kind of publicity. It is constantly emphasised by the Churches that clergymen and doctors must work as partners and not as rivals. Although it has been largely hidden, a ministry of healing has been practised in this country for the last fifty years. As late as the seventeenth century, however, healing was a recognised part of the Church's work. George Fox, the founder of the Society of Friends, frequently laid his hands on the sick and saw them recover. These miracles evoked no surprise. But the rationalism that held sway from the early eighteenth century onwards discouraged the practice of faith healing and it was allowed to lapse until a distinguished layman of the Church of England, Mr. J. M. Hickson, revived it. As a result of his friends' efforts the Committee on the Ministry of Healing, a Sub-Committee of the Lambeth Conference, of 1908, reported that in its opinion prayers for the restoration of health, which it recommended, might be fitly accompanied by the apostolic act of the laying on of hands.

After the First World War Mr. Hickson undertook a world tour in which he conducted religious services in the United States, Australia, New Zealand, Japan, China, India, and South Africa. He was welcomed by the clergy wherever he went. No trace of "hot gospelling" marked the services he conducted, but large crowds were attracted to hear him. They were encouraged to kneel at the altar rail, where Mr. Hickson laid his hands on their heads and prayed for them. He contended that any healing achieved was spiritual healing— the direct, immediate action of the Spirit of God upon his creatures. He urged all those who heard him to regard any curing of disease that his ministry effected as a sign of spiritual renewal and recreation. It might not be Christ's purpose to heal all who were sick, but he would assure all sufferers peace of mind and spiritual certainty.

Mr. Hickson found two notable disciples. One is Alderman the Rev. Jim Wilson, of the Guild of Health, and the other is the Rev. John Maillard, of the Christian Ministry of Healing at Milton Abbey, Dorset. At Milton Abbey it is argued that although some health movements are, from the Christian standpoint, on the wrong lines, they all combine as a challenge to the unbeliefs that God is the author of sickness and that

disease is part of the established order of things. It is held
by the Rev. Maillard and his fellow-workers that the value
of a ministry of healing lies in the fact that through it God
is restoring to men faith whereby they can live, and faith
whereby they can die; faith, also, whereby they can bear
others to die. This is typical of the British attitude in the
orthodox denominations to faith healing: the emphasis is on
the restoration to faith rather than on the restoration to
physical health.

All the same, it is held by those engaged in a ministry of
healing in this country that many and wonderful cures are
effected. They are not described as miracles, because, as Canon
Grensted was careful to point out in his Bampton lectures,
"Miracles of such a kind do not bear witness to the God of
Christianity, but to a sheer and terrifying disorder at the heart
of things. At the best they display a God Sultanic in character,
taking the one of two women grinding at the mill and leaving
the other, for no reason save that of his meaningless and
mysterious pleasure." Canon Grensted was markedly cautious
in his attitude to spiritual healing. He was a shrewd, though
fair, critic and he expressed many reservations in his acceptance
of such work. Even so, he admitted that when the worst had
been said such movements had opened the eyes of Christians
to new and immense possibilities inherent in faith. The
Churches' Council of Healing, an inter-denominational body
set up by the former Archbishop of Canterbury, Dr. William
Temple, was presently to go much further than this, for in
one of its reports it said that the Council deplored the frequent
use by doctors of the word "incurable" and added, "The
Christian doctor is coming more and more to regard it as
scientifically unsound to pronounce any illness incurable, and
is recognising the unseen factor of spiritual regeneration as
his greatest ally."

On the Churches' Council of Healing, as it is at present
constituted, there are official representatives from the British
Medical Association, the Church of England, the Episcopal
Church of Scotland, the Church of Ireland, the Methodist

Church, the Congregational Union, the Baptist Union, the Presbyterian Church of England, the Society of Friends, the Churches of Christ, and the Iona Community, as well as the Divine Healing Mission, the Guild of Health, and the Guild of St. Raphael. Its president is the Archbishop of Canterbury, its chairman the Bishop of Coventry, and its vice-chairman a Harley-street doctor. Among the members are the Bishops of Chichester and Lichfield, the Dean of St. Paul's, and at least a dozen doctors. The Spiritualist movement with its healers is not represented.

The Council's functions are to provide a common basis for those healing movements which stand on Christian foundations, drawing them into closer fellowship and co-operation; to provide a recognised basis for the co-operation of doctors and clergy in the study and performance of their respective duties in the work of healing; and to explore the possibilities of establishing common centres of healing under adequate medical and clerical supervision. Three points of agreement have been reached by those on the Council enabling these functions to be carried out. They are:

(1) All healing proceeds from the activity of the Eternal Creative power of God, ever seeking to restore harmony to his world. God's will for man is perfect health, but sickness and disease are facts which must be faced. Part of the victory of the Cross is the truth that suffering can be completely transformed by being offered to God and being taken up into the fellowship of Christ's redemptive sacrifice.

(2) God's infinite Power can work within His responsive creation to remake the whole human personality. Divine healing means essentially the healing of the whole man by the Power of God, through a clearer understanding of His Love and Purpose and in obedience to His Laws.

(3) Doctors, clergy and ministers are instruments of God's healing power in the faithful exercise of their skill and patience; and all members of the Churches can be used

by God for healing, through their ministry of prayer and intercession, meditation and direction; and through the sacraments and other means of grace.

The Council's report on its year's work published in 1951 affirmed that a growing number of Church of England clergymen were practising a healing ministry which they were accepting as part of their normal work and witness. The Bishop of Lincoln has appointed three of his clergy with a special commission to forward this work. The Lincoln Prayer Circle, which now has more than a hundred enrolled intercessors, formed into groups of ten, receives many requests for help given by prayer from all over the diocese. Regular monthly services of healing are conducted. Services of Intercession are also held from time to time in different churches, and a monthly corporate Communion Service, with special intention for the sick, is arranged. All this is in the one diocese of Lincoln, where this aspect of the Church's ministry, it is believed, is being richly blessed and is bringing the clergy into closer fellowship.

In Buckingham, the report continues, the clergy of Claydon Deanery sought the guidance of the Bishop concerning the work of divine healing. The Bishop replied that he had always held the view that there is ample scope for the exercise of a ministry of healing by every priest in his own parish, and that not half enough use is made of existing possibilities and privileges. The Bishop of Buckingham commended, as a valuable feature of parish life, the holding of a prayer circle or service for the sick in church "provided the whole setting is unostentatious and free of anything sensational. This may include from time to time the presence of such sick people who are able and willing to receive the laying-on-of-hands."

St. Martin-in-the-Fields holds a healing service at 3 p.m. on the first Wednesday in every month, when the congregation are linked in prayer with about 2,000 widely scattered invalids and prayer groups. These services are conducted jointly by an ordained clergyman and Mr. Godfrey Mowatt, a distinguished layman of the Church of England. At each service about thirty fresh names are entered in a specially compiled Book of Healing. The new names are passed to the congregation for their intercessory prayers; the old ones are the subject of an inclusive petition. The congregation are also given the names of those patients, sometimes numbering more than fifty, who have written during the month to express their thanks for the healing they have received as a result of the service. Finally, Mr. Mowatt, who is blind, stands in the sanctuary so that those who wish it may receive from him the ceremony of the laying on of hands. He emphasises that no one should regard him as a "healer", but if they come to him in faith for this ceremony they will receive new inspiration and understanding. When the mind has been recharged spiritually, spiritual regeneration, if it is the divine will, will come.

"The unobtrusive, selfless ministry of Mr. Godfrey Mowatt," states the report of the Churches' Council of Healing, "has done much during the past years to bring home the essential significance of Divine Healing to churchmen collectively and individually. His witness, based on the simple fact that the healed become Christ's channels of healing, raises the whole movement above surmise into the clear air of demonstrable truth. He demonstrates the power of the Holy Spirit to move through men to heal bodies as well as minds and spirits, and the essential simplicity of his message, and his approach to all forms of suffering, carries conviction that nothing can assail. What the movement owes to Mr. Mowatt's practical labours and inspiration is recognised by all who know him, but we would like to take this opportunity to place on record the gratitude of the very large number of people who have received during the past year God's healing and blessing at his hands."

The Divine Healing Mission of the Church of England has two branches, the Healer Prayer Circle Union and the Prayer Union for the Prevention and Healing of Mental Suffering. They are both active and are continually forming new groups. The Healer Prayer Circle Union has about 140 centres at home and throughout the Commonwealth. New Zealand is particularly strong. A new centre has been formed in Vancouver. The Prayer Union for the Prevention and Healing of Mental Suffering reports large numbers giving thanks for complete recovery from mental illness. This is particularly encouraging because of the difficulty of obtaining hospital treatment for these sufferers in the early stages of their sickness, following the flood of applications under the recent health measures. "It is hoped," says the Churches' Council, "that the immensity of the need of such sufferers will awaken many people to the call to take part in intercession on their behalf, through which the Healing Love and Mercy can be made manifest by the restoration of harmony and peace to distressed and distracted hearts and minds."

Other denominations are equally active in developing the work of healing through prayer. The number of prayer groups in the Methodist Connexion is increasing. The Spiritual Healing Fellowship of the Society of Friends has now twenty-four Prayer Groups, including one in Geneva. The Horsham Friends have been specially concerned with the needs of a number of mentally defective children, who have made, it is said, marked progress. A band of London Friends, whose members prayed for eighteen months for eleven patients in mental hospitals, was able to report to the Council that not one patient remained on their lists.

Among British Nonconformists no man has done more to advance spiritual healing than the Rev. Dr. Leslie Weatherhead. His approach has been mainly along the pathway of psychology. During the greater part of his ministry he has conducted psychotherapeutical clinics at which he has tried to heal many who were sick by adjusting body, mind, and spirit. An extension of these efforts is the Fellowship of Silence he conducts every Sunday evening at the City Temple. He has now worked out a technique of healing by prayer. He believes that one of the fundamental rules is that only about four or five cases can be lifted to God in prayer on any one evening, for it puts too great a strain on a congregation to ask people to steady their minds and hold them in intense prayer for the sick if they are asked to intercede for more. Dr. Weatherhead prefers to be able to name to his congregation the sufferer for whom they are asked to pray, and he likes to be able to describe in some detail what the patient is going through. In this way, he believes, it is possible to concentrate the power of prayer. He finds it is usually more effective if he can tell the congregation that the sufferer is, for example, a nurse aged twenty studying at a particular hospital, that she is the victim of tuberculosis perhaps, that her temperature is high, that she cannot sleep undrugged, and that she has not eaten for some time. The intercessors are asked to imagine that Christ is standing beside her bed touching her life, and that his healing power is at that moment being made manifest in her body. There is a momentary silence, and then Dr. Weatherhead says: "Please do not let your mind wander. Hold it steadily there, lifting up Miss X to God." Or he may say: "Let your prayers do what your arms would do if we lived in the days of Christ. We should carry the patient into his presence. Believe that your prayer is bringing the patient and Christ into living proximity and vital relationship." There is another interval of silence, and then he takes up the next case.

In a booklet he has written for the Methodist Conference, *Healing Through Prayer,* he has said that one nurse who was thus prayed for made a marvellous recovery. The girl did not know she was being prayed for, but her temperature at that very hour went down to normal. The next morning she began to take light food for the first time for some days. She is now, he says, a "radiant Christian".

Dr. Weatherhead holds that God will not magically make up for our laziness or ignorance. "Medicine and surgery and psychology are necessary," he writes. "We welcome them all. Everything that the mind of man can think out, or the hand of man devise, must be done to co-operate with God. And many people die because our co-operation with God on the physical side is not adequate or complete enough. We lose them, though we may comfort ourselves by thinking that God still has them in His keeping and in His plan." He desires to see in every church prayer-circles of which the members would be people of faith and devotion.

Dr. Harold Roberts, in another booklet for the Methodist Conference, *The Sanctions of Christian Healing,* has called for a new "technique" of faith healing. This, he argues, should be based on worship, prayer, the sacraments, and teaching. A Christian background to human life should be strengthened, he believes, so that faith in God may be awakened and sustained in the whole community. When this has been achieved there should be constructive co-operation with other ministries of healing, particularly medicine, surgery, and psychotherapy, by providing Christian healing centres for joint study and practice. Dr. Roberts also thinks there should be, at agreed intervals, a reverent and honest exploration of methods of faith healing to assess results.

Another medical man, Dr. Howard E. Collier, of the Society of Friends, has also thought carefully about the technique of prayer. He recommends that the first step is to see that the body is properly disposed for worship. Those who pray should assume a poised and balanced position of the body. Rigidity and slouching have equally to be avoided. Every muscle must be relaxed as fully as possible. The head must not be allowed to sink too far down and forward, and even the jaws and eyebrows must be carefully relaxed. Having prepared the body, the mind must be prepared, turning itself inwards towards its "quiet centre". Dr. Collier goes on, in a pamphlet he has written, *The Place of Spiritual Healing in the Society of Friends*: "If the thoughts stray (and stray they will) very gently shepherd them back towards their fold. At this stage it may help to hold in the mind some thought of wisdom, of beauty, of truth, or of goodness—an act of love or the remembered scent of hay in summer, or the sound of wind in the grasses on a sun-bathed hill. Thus we pass to controlled, not vacant, but 'centred' meditation which is the preparation for Worship." In this state, Dr. Collier believes, the "empty beaker" of the faithful is refilled by the Being of God. Only by a life of active well-doing, arising out of a worship-completed life, can this power be renewed in the life of Christ's healers.

Dr. Collier says he has seen, through the healing power of prayer, the chronic bedridden walk, "evil spirits cast out", and unexpected recoveries made from physical illness, operations, poisonings, heart diseases, blood pressure, and even growths. In his opinion, however, it is unwise to make extravagant assertions for spiritual healing. Instead, the sick should be encouraged to seek the "First Thing" first in the hope and confident expectation that a large measure of the other needful things like health will be "added unto them".

Let me now try to bring together all these many aspects of spiritual healing by focusing on one of these practitioners at work. For this purpose I choose the London Healing Mission, the headquarters of which are at Dawson Place, Bayswater, London, W.2. The Mission has now upwards of 2,000 members, of whom rather fewer than one in four are active intercessors. They are organised by the Rev. William Wood, a Church of England missioner. To each group of ten intercessors he sends the names of four or five sufferers every month. Like Dr. Leslie Weatherhead, the Rev. Wood believes it is too much to ask a group to pray for more than this number at a time. But the requests to be prayed for are greater than is the number of intercessors available. At the end of each month the names of those patients who are still ill are placed in the Book of Healing on which the missioner lays his hands as part of the weekly services. This practice accords with that at St. Martin-in-the-Fields.

The Mission's work has aroused so much interest that invitations are pouring in upon Mr. Wood to explain his methods to provincial churches. Before he holds a healing service elsewhere he asks that the congregation should be spiritually prepared. He believes that this is important. There may be two preliminary services before a healing service is arranged in a fresh church. Those who attend the chapel in Dawson Place are asked to read carefully a Preparation Paper which

Mr. Wood has written. This mentions that healing is a spiritual gift. God desires to make all men better so that they may enter into life in all its fullness. But first we must be cleansed from sin and be single-hearted in our desire to fulfil His Will. It is pointed out that although the services are extremely simple, they are not suitable for children. Parents are therefore asked to bring any child who needs help and healing to the church half an hour before the service, so that when they have received help they can be immediately taken home. Children who are timid or who ought not to leave home can be helped, it is said, in other ways than by attending the services.

The Preparation Paper says that the ministry is given in faith in the Healing Presence and the Power of Christ in and through his Church, in answer to prayer. The sick are asked to look forward to healing as a gift of God and to prepare for it in the same spirit as they would for any other of God's spiritual gifts and blessings. It is suggested that they should offer this prayer every day:

"Heavenly Father, I thank Thee for the gift of faith. Without the revelation of Thy Blessed Son Jesus Christ I could not know Thee or love Thee or have faith in Thee. He has awakened and inspired my faith. O God, increase my faith, and help my unbelief.

"I would humbly confess and readily forsake all my sins. Cleanse and pardon me: sanctify and guide me: keep me teachable and guidable; strengthen me that I may be sincere in my surrender to Thee and in forgiveness of others: fill me with Thy love.

"No one can deserve Thy healing. Life and Healing are Thy gifts of Love. Not in my worthiness but in Thy mercy do I put my trust. As a child of God I lift up my heart and hands to receive Thy blessing. In my thanksgiving I give myself to Thee to be more loving and obedient to Thy Will. In Thy compassion Thou dost have mercy upon my weakness, and dost heal me. It is Thy love which stoops to touch and bless me. Father I praise and thank Thee.

"Fill me anew with the Spirit of Jesus that my life may be changed and made anew. Then shall I seek Thy glory in all things and obey Thy Will. For Thy Holy Name's sake. Amen."

That prayer expresses the essence of the Mission's services.

Mr. Wood claims nothing for himself. "Miracles are not magic," he says. "Healing is not magic. Spiritual healing is the work of God. We must put our trust in Him and not in the minister, who has nothing of his own to give. All that the minister can do is to be faithful to God."

Every Thursday Mr. Wood holds services at Dawson Place. The times are 11 a.m., when Holy Communion is celebrated, 2.30 p.m. and 7 p.m. Thus no one is barred from attending a service at the Mission because of shift work or household duties.

The Mission's chapel has been beautifully constructed out of what was once the basement kitchen of a dwelling-house. There is no organ and no choir. Each service is followed by the ceremony of the laying on of hands, which is done according to high Anglican ritual. At the service I attended Mr. Wood read from a sheaf of letters he had received that morning from supplicants. One was from a woman who had taken two years to nerve herself to enter hospital. Now she asked for prayers for herself and for a Roman Catholic in her ward who was dangerously ill. There was a letter from a woman about to have an operation on her knee, and another letter was from a young man in Turkey who had heard of the Mission.

The chapel is so small that only a dozen people at a time can kneel at the altar rails for Mr. Wood to lay his hands upon their bowed heads and offer a whispered prayer for each in turn. At least forty sufferers that morning queued for places. There was utter silence and the deepest reverence. A feeling of power not of this world seemed to flow from the ministering priest in his white vestments.

A sense of the divine is conveyed in many ways. Moses saw it in the burning bush. Elijah heard it in the still small

F

voice that followed the earthquake and the fire. For my part, I caught a hint, a gleam of it that morning in the murmured prayers, the perfect stillness, and the hands of the minister gently laid on each suffering suppliant head beneath the Cross in that little chapel.

CHAPTER XI

WHAT THE SCEPTICS SAY

THE critics of Spiritualism form themselves into two main, and ostensibly diametrically opposed, groups—the materialists and the churchmen, especially Roman Catholics and High Anglicans. They do not make common cause in their attack on Spiritualism, for to do so would be paradoxical, since their onslaught is made from positions that are poles asunder. Both these groups of critics, however, strike hard at the Spiritualists' eager quest for "proofs" of survival after death. To both sets of opponents the apologists for Spiritualism believe they have complete answers. Remorseless controversy extending over eighty years has by now clearly determined the issues, so that the arguments, the cut and thrust of the debate, follow well-defined patterns. In this chapter I shall outline the chief criticisms that are levelled against Spiritualism and psychic research. These attacks I shall not attempt to answer, for this is not a work of propaganda. A detached objectivity is my aim. Since I have reported the claims made out by the Spiritualists and their allies, it is but scant justice that I should present the sceptics' case so that the reader may be helped to form his own opinion. Should he desire to learn *how* Spiritualists reply to their opponents' objections I recommend him to consult their publicists—he will not find them silent.

Let us begin with those Churchmen who object to the practice of Spiritualism.

The Roman Catholic Church forbids any attempt at communication with the dead explicitly and absolutely. This has always been its attitude. It bases its teaching about this on Biblical authority, citing both the Old and the New Testaments. The text in the Old Testament that is most frequently quoted in this connection occurs in the eighteenth chapter of Deuteronomy: "There shall not be found among you any one that maketh his son or his daughter to pass through the fire, or that useth divination, or an observer of times, or an enchanter, or a witch, or a charmer, or a consulter with familiar spirits, or a wizard, or a necromancer. For all that do these things are an abomination unto the Lord: and because of these abominations the Lord thy God doth drive them out from before thee." Nevertheless the Church does firmly preach without the slightest equivocation the resurrection of the dead. It gives cogent support to this cardinal tenet by its doctrine of the immortality of the saints, whom it continues in this age to canonise from time to time.

Father Herbert Thurston, the Jesuit, in his defence of the Church's attitude towards Spiritualism, pointed out that she did not make up her mind hastily. Spiritualism had been practised for fifty years before the Holy Office in 1898 forbade Catholics to experiment with automatic writing and to use the planchette, the ouija board, and all such devices. Nineteen years then elapsed before another pronouncement was made. This ostracised Spiritualism for all Roman Catholics in these strong and unambiguous terms:

"It is unlawful to assist at any spiritistic utterances or manifestations whatever, whether through a medium or without one, even if these utterances or manifestations bear the appearance of propriety and piety; whether this assistance lies in interrogating souls or spirits or listening to the replies, or merely in looking on, and even though there be a tacit or expressed protestation of not intending any intercourse with evil spirits."

This doctrine stands. It has not, so far as I know, ever been amended. Even so, the Roman Catholic Church does permit, under strictly regulated conditions, research into psychic matters by those whom she jealously licenses for this purpose. One of those allowed to conduct psychic research has been the Spanish Jesuit, Father C. M. de Heredia, who began by denouncing all psychical manifestations as fraudulent and then later found himself compelled to modify this view. Another Catholic researcher is the Dominican, Father Mainage, professor of the History of Religions at the Paris Catholic Institute. He too has written in a booklet, *La Religion Spirite*, that he believes in the objectivity of spiritualistic phenomena. "There are tables which turn and which talk," Father Mainage writes. "Mediumistic script is not the figment of a crazy imagination. Apparitions are not all of them the results of unreal hallucinations, and the partial materialisations obtained by Dr. Geley are not a pure chimera." Yet another Jesuit, Father Alois Gatterer, a professor at Innsbruck University, sat with a famous Austrian medium of the 'twenties, Rudi Schneider, and afterwards defended the reality of the psychical phenomena he saw. All this is frankly admitted by the late Father Thurston in the booklet on *Spiritualism* which he wrote for the Catholic Truth Society.

The three Catholic investigators mentioned were all genuine students of psychic matters. They were theologians who knew enough psychology in the Church's eyes to be able to observe the phenomena they saw scientifically, and so they were permitted to sit with mediums and attend seances. On all others, however honest their intentions, the Church imposes the unflinching ban I have quoted, and she does this on the ground that to dabble in psychic matters is dangerous, as Spiritualists themselves clearly recognise, because of the possibility of demoniac possession leading to madness, immorality, and even suicide. Father Thurston was a severe critic of Spiritualism. He admitted the increasing modern interest in psychical phenomena, and he attributed this to a loss of faith in Christian revelation. He rejected the doctrines of Spiritualism concerning the nature of the "other world" because, in his view, these doctrines are based "upon the word of such purporting communicators as Red Cloud, White Feather, Imperator, Nona, Joannes, Moonstone, and a crowd of others for whose existence in this world or the next not a shadow of evidence is forthcoming beyond the fact that these are the fantastic names they have chosen to give themselves".

Other Catholic opponents of Spiritualism have argued that the souls of the dead are in the hands of God, whether they are in heaven, or hell, or purgatory. If God permits them to communicate with the living, well and good; it is the divine will. But attempts by the living to establish communication are, in Roman Catholic opinion, idle and sinful. Those who have doubts concerning human survival—doubts which are to the Catholic irrational and sinful—should dispel them by means of prayer and meditation. Some Catholic critics have asserted that any intelligences that give communications at Spiritualistic seances must normally be those of either the damned or of demons with whom it is mortally sinful to satisfy curiosity by holding intercourse. This charge has aroused pain and offence among Spiritualists who fiercely repudiate it.

Dr. Richard Downey, the Archbishop of Liverpool, reinforced the Roman Catholic criticism of Spiritualism with psychological reasons in a preface he contributed in 1944 to Father H. V. O'Neill's book on *Spiritualism*. The Archbishop argued that the statements of trance-mediums can frequently be explained by the ordinary psychoanalytic principles for interpreting dreams. Dreams to the psychoanalyst are symbols for the fulfilment of a repressed wish. "The utterances of trance-mediums," Dr. Downey wrote, "abound in instances of desires fulfilled. Because the medium in his waking state wishes that there should be no hell and no suffering in 'the beyond', the dream consciousness asserts that there is none. . . . Because Sir Arthur Conan Doyle was an advocate of easier divorce his mediums very naturally assure him that 'on the other side' spirits dwell in groups, but only 'affinitized' spirits are together, husbands and wives in many cases being astral miles apart. Because Sir Oliver Lodge was interested in physics his mediums tell him how bricks are manufactured in spirit-land, and how the essence of terrestrial clothes passes over and is woven into spirit-clothes on etherial looms. A spirit hypothesis of any kind seems hardly necessary to account for 'such stuff as dreams are made on'."

Dr. Downey continued his attack by quoting a statement of Dr. Quackenbos in a book, *Body and Spirit,* that the writer had never heard a medium say anything that could not be accounted for by the theory of thought-transference and that he had never seen a medium do anything that could not be rationally explained as due to the action of supersensible psychic force. The Archbishop similarly quotes Jung's theory that ghostly "apparitions" are entirely subjective experiences— "the result of a crisis," he wrote, "in the internecine strife that goes on unceasingly deep down in the unconsciousness of each one of us between the ego-complex and the constellation of complexes around it and inimical to it." Dr. Downey added that there is no end to the psychological theories which have been devised to account for abnormal psychical occurrences. He admitted, however, that even so there remained a residue of unexplained psychical phenomena, and he suggested that this might possibly be accounted for as due to Satanic intervention. It was for this reason that the Church had laid down certain definite theological principles. Her teaching is that good and evil spirits do exist, and are able to communicate with man, subject to God's sanction. This sanction is given positively in the case of good spirits; the communications of evil spirits God merely tolerates. The Church, Dr. Downey declared, finds "strong presumptive evidence" that the communications passed in the seance room are of diabolic origin. She therefore condemns Spiritualism on the theological principle that it is wrong to communicate with evil spirits. "As to whether diabolic intervention takes place in any particular case the Church pronounces no judgment," the Archbishop wrote. "That is a question of fact to be decided on the evidence. But whether in any particular case there be Satanic intervention or not makes no difference with regard to the culpability of attending the seance. The Catholic who attends does a thing which the Church in her wisdom has forbidden in the gravest possible manner."

The teaching of the Church of England concerning Spiritualism is by no means easy to elicit, and this also applies to many of the Nonconformist denominations. Generally the practice is to allow freedom of conscience to their followers, which accords, of course, with their Protestant inclination. It is noteworthy that many prominent clergymen, from the time of the Rev. Stainton Moses to our own day, have openly associated with Spiritualist groups. Others have been members of the Society for Psychical Research. Some Churchmen, especially High Anglicans, refuse, however, to have anything to do with Spiritualism. This applies especially where divine healing is carried on as part of the Christian ministry. The gulf between divine healers and Spiritualist healers is often wide and deep. The toleration shown by some Churchmen and the opposition displayed by others makes it difficult, even impossible, to say precisely what is the doctrine of the Church of England concerning Spiritualism.

In 1937 Dr. Cosmo Gordon Lang, when he was Archbishop of Canterbury, appointed a commission of eleven members to investigate the subject of communications with discarnate spirits and the claims of Spiritualism in relation to the Christian faith. The chairman of the commission, which sat for two years gathering its evidence, was Dr. Francis Underhill, a former Dean of Rochester and afterwards Bishop of Bath and Wells. At the end of the inquiry it submitted a report to the Archbishop, who then circulated it among the bishops of the Church of England. That report has never been published officially, despite urgent pressure to do so from the Spiritualists. In reply to their agitation they were informed that it had been decided that further investigation was necessary and that premature publication would be liable to give rise to misunderstanding. Whether that additional investigation has been concluded and what its nature has been is not known. The Spiritualists assert that a majority report, agreeing that their case for survival after death has been made out, was signed by Dr. Underhill, Canon H. Ansom, Master of the Temple; Dr. W. R. Matthews, Dean of St. Paul's; Canon L. W. Grensted; Dr. William Brown, the psychologist; Mr. P. E. Sandilands, K.C.; and Lady Gwendolen Stephenson.

The other three members of the commission, so the Spiritualists say, signed a minority report. These statements have never been categorically denied, nor have summaries purporting to outline the commission's majority report ever been challenged on material points. There is still no official statement from the Church of England concerning the tenets of Spiritualism, though the Commission on Christian Doctrine has reported that to believe positively in the existence of spiritual beings other than human is in no way irrational. This is not, of course, a pronouncement on Spiritualistic doctrine.

The situation is different north of the Border, because the Church of Scotland conducted more than thirty years ago an independent inquiry into Spiritualism. This was done after the Rev. William A. Reid, of Glasgow, had petitioned the General Assembly to investigate psychic phenomena. At the end of the inquiry the Church decided, said Dr. Norman MacLean, an ex-Moderator, that psychical research did not conflict with the teachings of the Christian faith. Accordingly no ban was imposed on members of the Church exercising their minds in this field. "The present position of the Church of Scotland," the Rev. William Reid said, "is that ministers and laymen have a perfect right, if they please, to investigate psychic phenomena and to believe that human survival is now proved." This does not imply, of course, that the Church of Scotland accepts the theology developed in Spiritualist churches; that is another matter altogether. But the survival hypothesis and the right to investigate it are freely conceded.

Not every Spiritualist, it should be emphasised, desires to break away from his accustomed church. Many who frequent Spiritualist services do so for the sake of the mediumship and in the hope of receiving a personal message from the other side. Such people as these disregard, perhaps are never aware of, the Spiritualistic theology. Lord Dowding, for example, one of the most powerful propagandists on behalf of Spiritualism writing today, still regards himself as a member of the Church of England. He says that the atmosphere of his own parish church is more congenial to him than that of other denominations.

That distinguished Churchman, Dr. W. R. Inge, the former Dean of St. Paul's, repudiates the survival hypothesis on grounds that are typical of his scholarly mind. "Ghost-stories have no attraction for the Platonist," Dr. Inge wrote in *The Philosophy of Plotinus*. "He does not believe in them. The kind of immortality which 'psychical research' endeavours to establish would be for him a negation of the only immortality which he desires or believes in. The difference between the two hopes is fundamental. Some men are so much in love with what Plotinus would call the lower soul-life, the surface consciousness and surface-experience which make up the content of our sojourn here as known to ourselves, that they wish, if possible, to continue it after their bodies are mouldering in the grave. Others recognise that this lower soul-life is a banishment from the true home of the Soul, which is in a supra-temporal world, and they have no wish to prolong the conditions of their probation after the probation itself is ended, and we are quit of our 'body of humiliation'."

From the criticisms of Churchmen we turn now to the criticisms of materialists. To them the Universe is explainable in terms of matter and motion. All psychical processes, they argue, can be accounted for as being due to chemical and physical changes in the nervous system. Such theories have, during the last one hundred years, appealed strongly to men trained in science. The evolutionary hypothesis of Natural Selection appeared to make nonsense of fundamental religious concepts. It is true that Darwin, in *The Origin of Species*, did concede the existence of a Divine Creator, but he argued that this Being was subject to His own laws. "To my mind," Darwin wrote, "it accords better with what we know of the laws impressed on matter by the Creator, that the production and extinction of the past and present inhabitants of the world should have been due to secondary causes like those determining the birth and death of the individual. . . . There is a grandeur in this view of life, with its several powers, having been originally breathed by the Creator into a few forms or into one; and that, whilst this planet has gone cycling on according to the fixed laws of gravity, from so simple a beginning endless forms most beautiful and most wonderful have been, and are being evolved."

Thus Darwin. Later scientists, however, readily dispensed with the notion of a Creator. They argued that life itself, and after life then mind, must have evolved from matter. Latterly Mr. Fred Hoyle, the Cambridge astronomer and mathematician, has pressed this philosophy to its logical conclusion. Mr. Hoyle believes in the spontaneous generation of matter, formed out of trailing clouds of hydrogen, in a continually expanding Universe. Mr. Hoyle popularly expounded his cosmology in a famous series of broadcast lectures, *The Nature of the Universe,* which startled thousands of listeners because of the force of the materialist argument he presented. In his summing-up Mr. Hoyle said: "It seems to me that religion is but a blind attempt to find an escape from the truly dreadful situation in which we find ourselves. Here we are in this truly fantastic Universe with scarcely a clue as to whether our existence has any real significance." Naturally his forthright scepticism aroused considerable controversy. Other thinkers, including some astronomers, came forward to refute him. But if he is right, then Spiritualism, along with all religion promising immortality, must be dismissed as superstition, unless it be conceived, and no philosopher has yet stated this hypothesis, that an immortal spirit in man has been spontaneously generated at some point in history.

Some materialists hold that the mind is only to be understood in terms of the body. If the body is well then the mind will be healthy, but if one part of the body—the brain—is diseased then insanity inevitably follows. Other parts of the body—the glands, for example—similarly condition the human character, and upon them depends the true essence of each individual. The inmost nature of a man, these materialists argue, derives from his thyroid or the quantity of iodine in his body. Here again, if they are right, there can be no soul, no spirit, to survive death. These doctrines, however, are not accepted by such recent philosophers as Bergson, Alexander, and Lloyd Morgan, who have taught that a strictly materialistic and mechanistic interpretation of the Universe cannot cover all the known facts and that there are other forces in Nature which must be recognised.

Other materialists dismiss Spiritualism for what they believe to be practical reasons. They argue that the alleged communication with the dead has never allowed Schubert, for example, to complete the *Unfinished Symphony,* Dickens to supply the solution to the mystery of *Edwin Drood,* nor Stevenson to tell us the end he had planned for *Weir of Hermiston.* These critics assert that the bulk of the messages supposed to have come from the dead have dealt with the merest trivialities, and that nothing purporting to describe the nature of existence beyond the grave is anything more than elementary Utopianism. Twenty-five years ago Mr. A. A. Milne wrote in a newspaper article that the "other life" described by Spiritualists was a mixture of a Boy Scouts' Saturday afternoon and a gathering of the clans in a world which might have been designed by an energetic Town Council slightly under the influence of Mr. Edmund Dulac. Intellectual aversion of this type is enough to prompt many people to reject the Spiritualist hypothesis of survival after death.

Materialists frequently denigrate the intellectual capacity of those who accept the "evidence" of survival, and they do not hesitate to belittle the reputations of the most distinguished men and women who have accepted the Spiritualists' case. Thus it is said of Marshall Hall that he won his cases because of his emotionalism rather than his grasp of law; that Conan Doyle was converted to Spiritualism when his literary and mental powers were declining, as the deterioration of his Sherlock Holmes stories showed; that Sir William Crookes, for all his standing as a scientist, was credulous and unworldly in business affairs; and that Professor Sir William Barrett was so willing to accept any phenomena labelled psychic that he even advised his pupils to use a divining rod to discover beforehand whether they were going to pass their examinations. One by one the reputations of the greatest people who have embraced Spiritualism are by this method whittled away.

Another line of attack emphasises that the testimonies, however honestly advanced, of those who have had "evidence" from the other world are all individual statements that have never, as they would be if offered in a court of law, been subjected to trained examination and cross-examination and then pronounced upon by those expert in the nature of evidence. The frauds known to have been perpetrated by some mediums in the past are constantly cited, and the critic of this type rarely fails to point to self-deception and heterodeception as the true explanation of "psychic phenomena". We are reminded, what can scarcely be denied, that human beings are only too ready to believe what they wish to believe.

Some scientific materialists, for the most part biologists, assert that what is supposed to be the human soul or spirit can have no separate entity when divorced from the body. This appears to beg the question unashamedly. But these critics hold that body and soul form a unity, and that when one dies so does the other. The living body, it is contended, is but a complex of chemical and electrical phenomena. And the question is asked why, if man is supposed to have an immortal soul, the same is not true of all that is alive in Nature —animals, fishes, microbes, flowers, and vegetation? Spiritualists, as we noticed in Chapter V, appear to be reluctant to admit more than a few beloved animals, mostly pets, to their heaven.

Most materialists join with the Churchmen who oppose Spiritualism in pointing to the dangers of psychic experiment, though they do so largely for different reasons. They cannot logically assert the perils of demoniac possession, because they do not believe in demons, but they reiterate how often dabbling in occult matters has led to insanity. Psychic research has been denounced as spiritual drug-taking inasmuch as it is alleged to weaken the ability of those who undertake it to cope with everyday realities and to destroy a sane outlook on life. It may lead, it has sometimes been argued, to blackmail. A few critics have berated Spiritualism as a grave social menace that tends to vitiate the beauty of life while promoting neuroses and superstition.

Professor Joseph Jastrow, the psychologist, of Wisconsin University, was one of Spiritualism's most uncompromising critics. In his article on "The Animus of Psychical Research" contributed to *The Case For and Against Psychical Belief*, published in America in 1927, he argued that what believers regarded as evidence of survival was the product of prepossession. "Each mind resorts," Jastrow stated, "to the legitimate concepts of science, physical, biological, mechanical, to give the conclusions the appearance, really the pathetic travesty of a scientific demonstration, but ever with an underlying animus that nullifies and is wholly incompatible with the most elementary allegiance to science and logic alike." This vitiating "animus" displayed, in Professor Jastrow's opinion, by Spiritualists and psychic researchers, lies, he believed, in the pursuit of the psychical for its personal significance. He held that this animus is seen in the attempt at proving there are psychic phenomena in Nature that transcend the ordinary operations recognised in the field of psychology; that this animus is inherent in the belief that there are mediums and sensitive individuals who possess psychic gifts; and, finally, that it is revealed when interest is shown in a world differently regulated, motivated, and directed than the one in which we conduct our daily lives and occupations. Sometimes, Jastrow alleged, this animus is passed off as mysticism; at other times it can be detected in a preoccupation with prophetic dreams, divinations, and premonitions. Dreams, he admitted, are a proper study for psychological purposes, but to believe in dreams as prophetic or veridical is, he asserted, to inject this treacherous psychical animus. "The same applies," he wrote, "to the veridical, the vague 'something in it' attitude of ordinary conversation which places the 'something' in a system apart from the naturalistic ones, which includes the psychological interpretation of pre-monitions as a combination of coincidence, community of mental habit, and allied procedures, and refers divination to subconsciously directed indications.

"The tendency to the 'third order of knowledge' is largely a search for an aesthetic satisfaction; to yield to it makes a more interesting, personally significant world, breaks the routine of the humdrum, and adds a charm as well as a dimension to existence. And its harm? If not carried too far and to the sacrifice of normal activities and pragmatically stable beliefs, doubtless in many instances, slight, though never negligible, and in the extreme disintegrating. With a world so thoroughly rationalised and humanitarianised as ours, the menace is much reduced. But science is too precious a social inheritance to be toyed with, and certainly to be challenged by the psychological limitations of our rationality."

The late Harry Houdini, a professional escapologist who was known as "the handcuff king", was another complete sceptic of the survival hypothesis on the grounds that he had learned of no mediumistic phenomena during many years devoted to the study of Spiritualism that he himself could not repeat by methods know to conjurers. He believed that many of those who sit with mediums are devoid of any ability to observe acutely—a defect which, in his opinion, allowed mediums to accomplish apparent miracles when in reality they were cleverly misguiding and aptly misdirecting the attention of their sitters. Houdini boasted that he had never been baffled in the least by anything he had seen at seances. Everything he had witnessed had been merely a form of mystification. He held that the secret of all such "performances", as he called them, is to catch the mind off guard and the moment after it has been surprised to con-tinue with something else that carries the intelligence along with the performer, even against the spectator's will. Even men of the intellectual calibre of Sir William Crookes, W. T. Stead, Sir Oliver Lodge, and Sir Arthur Conan Doyle had, he believed, been deceived by this technique. Because he himself was proof against it all his sittings with mediums had been negative.

"What would be more wonderful to me than to be able to converse with my beloved mother?" Houdini wrote in "A Magician Among the Mediums" contributed to *The Case For and Against Psychical Belief*. "Surely there is no love in this world like a mother's love, no closeness of spirit, no other heart throbs that beat alike; but I have not heard from my blessed Mother, except through the dictates of the inmost recesses of my heart, the thoughts which fill my brain and the memory of her teachings.

"Would not my private secretary, John William Sargent, come back to me and tell me the secrets of the beyond if it were possible? Did he not, just before he died, tell me that he would come to me if there was any way of doing it? More than being a private secretary, he was my friend—true, loyal, sacrificing—knew me for thirty years. He has not come back to me and he would if it were possible.

"I had compacts with a round dozen. Each one promised me faithfully to come back to me if it were possible. I have even gone so far as to create secret codes and hand-grips. Sargent had a certain word he was to repeat to me; William Berol, the eminent mental specialist, gave me the secret hand-shake a few hours before he died and did not regain consciousness after silently telling me that he remembered our compact; Atlanta Hall, niece of President Pierce, a woman ninety years of age, who had had seances with the greatest mediums that visited Boston, called for me just before her death, clasped my hand and gave me our agreed-upon grip which she was to give me through a medium. They have never come back to me! Does that prove anything? I have attended a number of seances since their death, the mediums have called for them, and when their spirit forms were supposed to appear, not one of them could give me the proper signal. Would I have received it? I'll wager I would have. There was love of some kind between each of these friends who are gone and myself. It is needless to point out the love of a mother and son; the love of a real friend; the love of a woman of ninety toward a man who held her dear; the love of a philosopher toward a man who respected his life study—they were all loves, each strong, each binding. If these persons, with all the love they bore in their heart for me and all the love I have in my heart for them, did not return, what about those who did not hold me close, who had no interest in me? Why should they come back and mine not?"

Houdini concluded with this charge: "If Spiritualism is to be founded on the tricks of exposed mediums, feats of magic, resort to trickery, then I say unflinchingly I do not believe, and more, I will not believe. I have said many times that I am willing to believe, want to believe, will believe if the spiritualists can show any substantiated proof, but until they do I shall have to live on, believing from all the evidence shown to me and from what I have experienced that Spiritualism has not been proven satisfactorily to the world at large and that none of the evidence offered has been able to stand up under the fierce rays of investigation."

Houdini was by no means the only expert "magician" who has proclaimed he could exactly counterfeit all that is ever supposed to have taken place in the seance room. One body of conjurors in Britain has been making for nearly forty years its own investigation of phenomena variously termed psychical, spiritualistic, metaphysical, paranormal, and parapsychological. During these inquiries it has from time to time exposed fraudulent mediums, but it alleges it has never once found an instance of a genuine phenomenon deemed to have been produced under rigorous test conditions. This group is pledged to publicise all such instances when discovered. It shrewdly criticised the methods of "spirit photographers" who enjoyed a vogue some twenty-five years ago; little is heard of "spirit" photography today. It has repeated levitations such as those which D. D. Home is supposed to have practised at the birth of Spiritualism nearly a century ago; and although it has inquired into numerous poltergeist stories it reports that it has never yet come across a genuine poltergeist. Generally, the group says, the phenomena have ceased after the investigators have visited the scene. These investigators state that they are not out of sympathy with Spiritualism. On the contrary, they say they have the greatest respect for its adherents. They assert they have an open mind on all matters connected with the supernatural. But their avowed enemy is the charlatan who deceives normally sensible people into believing he is endowed with powers he has no right to claim. And they state roundly that their investigations into psychic phenomena in many fields have all produced the same result—negative.

This, then, is the manifold case against Spiritualism broadly defined. I present it for the reader to judge it as he will. I shall make no attempt to refute it. Perhaps refutation is not possible, for the Churchmen who oppose Spiritualism and the materialists who reject it manifestly cannot both be right. If Spiritualism and faith healing, precognitive telepathy and extra-sensory perception require a defence there are regiments of men and women far better qualified than I am to supply it, and I am confident they will not be slow to speak up. But there is still one omission in this book that I must repair. It is now time to declare my own point of view so that the reader may correct for himself any bias that may have crept unwittingly into this effort to place in perspective our present knowledge of the further reaches of the mind.

CHAPTER XII

A SUMMING UP

THIS book has covered, all too rapidly perhaps, an immense amount of ground. It began by attempting to place modern psychic research and Spiritualistic practice in its historical setting. An assessment was then made of the strength of the Spiritualist movement and the varied activities of its adherents were sketched. We have moved from seances in darkened rooms to the light and quiet of the library of the Society for Psychic Research. Some of the current laboratory work of the parapsychologists has been studied. We have watched healing by Spiritualism and healing by prayer. We have seen devils cast out in consulting rooms and Obsession Circles. I have described how I have talked to the "dead".

From all this gathering of information I have emerged with certain opinions. These are, I freely admit, tentative, cloudy, and crude, for I have only scratched the surface in these studies, but still they have a core hard enough for the mind to grip.

Let me say at once that one effect of my inquiry has been to increase considerably my respect for Spiritualists. They are not the cranks I had once imagined them to be, nor, in Isaiah's phrase, "wizards that peep and that mutter". That statement stands and is not to be qualified. If I remain unconvinced, as yet, of the truth of "survival" and even criticise what I consider to be certain weaknesses of the movement that is another matter entirely. It may be presumptuous of me to make these criticisms, when still far from learned in psychic matters, but it is important, I think, that I should state them to acquaint the reader with my own habits of thought and thus permit him to make allowance for any errors of prejudice that may have unconsciously coloured my reporting.

I share the attitude of tolerance and sympathy that most Protestants nowadays are willing to accord to Spiritualists. Had I been a member of Parliament when the Witchcraft Act was debated I would have voted for its repeal. In adopting this attitude we appear to have stepped back three hundred years. In the seventeenth century John Donne, poet and Dean of St. Paul's, could write, believing in the literal truth of his words:

> *At the round earth's imagin'd corners, blow*
> *Your trumpets, Angels, and arise, arise*
> *From death, you numberless infinities*
> *Of souls, and to your scatter'd bodies go.*

And a little later, George Fox, the founder of the Society of Friends, could write of Margaret Rouse's dead child, as his *Book of Miracles* tells: "The Spirit of the child appeared to me and there was a mighty substance of a glorious life in that child, and I bid her mother be content, for it was well." Then came two centuries of rationalism, during which the teaching of a life after death was scoffed at and Hell, if not Heaven, obliterated. Now, however, Roman Catholics, Protestants, and some men of science are all willing to believe in personal survival in another life.

But one thing I deplore about Spiritualism is the quality of its literature. This is astonishingly poor. Why this should be I cannot explain. Spiritualism has produced an abundance of books, but few of real merit. Apart from the Rev. Stainton Moses's *Spirit Teachings*, still after three-quarters of a century the "Bible" of Spiritualism, the testimony of the movement continues to be written largely in the clichés of the Little Bethel. As one critic of Spiritualism put it to me: "The odd thing is that the messages which come through from the other world might all have been written by a sentimental curate." A similar point of view was expressed from within the movement when, after sitting with a medium, we began to converse about Spiritualism generally and he burst out: "I *know* there is no death as we understand it. But how to convince others? What this movement needs is a body of intellectuals." I admit that metaphysics appeal only to the sophisticated, and that the bulk of those who attend Spiritualist churches are not, by any stretching of terms, to be described as highbrows. They are, I expect, entirely satisfied with the standards of the Spiritualist books they read. But I contend that the movement would be all the stronger if within the corpus of its literature there were books of a more robust intellectual content.

There is, however, a passage in the Rev. Drayton Thomas's *Life Beyond Death*, a book which is certainly far above the average Spiritualist writing, that helps to explain why so many messages from the other world seem trivial and couched in inadequate language. The controlling spirit has, he explains, to use some of the medium's mind and also some of his own. There is thus a co-operation between spirit-mind and human-mind. The spirit control uses as much of its mind as it is able to, but its situation is something like having to turn from a full compass piano to perform for a time upon one having but a single octave of notes. Thus the limitations of the medium restrict the quality and nature of the communications.

One question over which I disagree with the Spiritualists concerns the possibility of telepathy being responsible for some of their most extraordinary successes. I have heard Mr. Ralph Rossiter, secretary of the Marylebone Spiritualist Association, relate, at a Sunday evening service of that body, two instances of information supplied by a medium that could not, he said, have been in the mind of the sitter at the time. The first instance concerned his wife, who was not at that time a Spiritualist. Overwrought by the death of her brother, she was persuaded to go to a Spiritualist church at Paignton, in Devon, where Mrs. Bertha Harris, a well-known medium, was demonstrating. Mrs. Harris described the dead man accurately and added: "He tells me your sister is with him." Mrs.

Rossiter at once denied that she had ever had a sister and
said she was sure she would have known if she had. "He says
your sister passed on just before you were born," Mrs. Harris
maintained. "Her name was Edith. Your brother says you
are to ask your mother, who can confirm this." Immediately
Mrs. Rossiter reached home she taxed her mother, who said
she had always been careful to suppress the fact of her child's
death and was surprised that it should have come out. I do
not doubt the authenticity of that story. I have the highest
respect for Mr. Rossiter's probity. To me it is inconceivable
that he would forward a story that was not completely
accurate. But we know from the work done by Whately
Carington, Soal, and Rhine on telepathy that this faculty
frequently skips across time and seems to anticipate the future.
This so-called "displacement" is mentioned in Chapter III of
this book. And so the doubt is left lingering in my mind
whether Mrs. Harris's message for Mrs. Rossiter may not have
been another instance of "displaced" telepathy.

The second instance Mr. Rossiter gave was even more extraordinary. The medium in question had been Mr. William
Redmond. At an M.S.A. service about a year previously he
had described to a woman in the congregation her dead
husband and added this message: "He wants you to know
that when your birthday comes round he will send you a red
carnation." The promise was certainly a surprising one. I
suppose that had I heard it at the time I should have thought
that the medium was "chancing his arm" knowing that carna-
tions are often bestowed as birthday gifts, though if one did
not materialise no great disappointment would result. But the
sequel, as Mr. Rossiter told it, was altogether fantastic. Six
months after the promise was given the widow had gone to
Bournemouth for her holidays. Her birthday had occurred
during her stay, and on it she had occasion, so she told
Rossiter afterwards, to travel by bus. She sat facing an empty
seat. Presently an old man sat down beside her. Next a
youth entered and sat in the empty seat opposite. He had
a red carnation in his buttonhole. When he got up to

leave the bus he glanced at the old man and said: "Say, you look a bit down in the mouth. Here—take my carnation. It may cheer you up." The old man looked at the flower, fondled it for a moment, and then turned to the widow beside him. "This is no use to me," he murmured. "I grow the things. You'd better have it," and handed it to her. Rossiter ended his story by asking how had the spirits managed to arrange the complex chain of effort by which that incident was brought about? And again I am left wondering whether it was not another example of "displaced" telepathy. I am unaware that the telepathists, with their scrupulously controlled experiments, have ever recounted a parallel instance of a lag of six months between the thing foreseen and its fulfilment. But once having admitted that displacement does sometimes take place, I cannot bring myself completely to rule it out. The doubt, a small one, persists, nagging me like sand in the shoe.

Even so, all who cherish the things of the spirit must be grateful to the Spiritualists for what they have done to force on our attention, in face of the strongest opposition, the possibility that life survives death.

Then there are the impressive achievements of prayer in curing sickness to which a large part of this book has been devoted. Those achievements are not to be brushed aside, although their explanation may still be doubtful. Are they due to divine intervention, as the Christian therapists contend? Or to the efforts of the spirits of Lister, Pasteur, or Red Indian medicine men, as the Spiritualists believe? Is hypnosis responsible? Or can the sicknesses that have yielded to these unorthodox healers merely be forms of hysteria that have passed, and with them the disabilities, once sympathy and attention had been given to the sufferers? I do not know. But I am disturbed that conventional medicine should be doing so little to explore the wisdom or otherwise of calling in the faith-healer. All too callously, or so it seems to one outside the medical profession, the surgeon and the physician pronounce sentence of death upon a patient and then wash their hands of him. Without a tremor, so soon as they come to the end of their knowledge, they label a morbid condition "incurable" and never question the assumption that their judgment is infallible. The faith healer admits no such limit to his work. "We dare not limit the power of God," Mrs. Elsie Salmon confidently cries, and she and her kind extend welcoming arms to those who have been consigned to Death. It is the same with Mr. Harry Edwards and the rest of the Spiritualist healers. If it is true, as they assert, that they have all conquered Death again and again and again, why are not the doctors calling in their aid for the sake of suffering humanity?

Occasionally, as we have seen, medical men both here and in America have testified to the power of prayer to cure diseases which they recognised to be beyond their skill to help. There are also Roman Catholic doctors who, when all else has failed, have encouraged their patients to seek a miracle at some shrine, such as Lourdes. At Lourdes the medical bureau is scrupulously careful to claim no case as a cure until it has been meticulously investigated. Even so such "miracles" are asserted from time to time. I am not aware that any similar inquiry is carried out by doctors concerning the results said to have been achieved by Spiritualist healers. For my part I am forced to believe, in face of the evidence I have found, that the Spiritualists do sometimes accomplish quite extraordinary things. Because I am still unconvinced of the truth of the central Spiritualist doctrine of survival, I have to add that these cures, which I accept, must be brought about by some other agency than "Spirits", such as suggestibility and the power of the mind in certain circumstances over the flesh. It may even be that the Spiritualists are right. I merely say that I am still open to conviction, in the same way as I remain open to conviction that the Christian therapists' explanation, that their cures are to be attributed to divine intervention, is the true one. Despite these hesitancies, however, I do hold most strongly that the impressive body of evidence of "miracle" cures must buttress the growing contemporary belief that notions long discarded about "soul" and "spirit" may not after all be so very far off the mark.

Having said this, I shall not be misunderstood, I hope, if I add that prayer and faith, thus applied, may have at times their own especial dangers. It may be, to put it crudely, that plagues and epidemics are manifestations of the Divine Will which calls for science, and not prayer, to meet them. A substantial part of the Old Testament is devoted to stringent laws of diet and social hygiene adapted to the well-being of a pastoral people living in the Middle East two thousand and more years ago. Those laws were broken by the people for whom they were devised only at the peril of their lives. If sickness and disaster followed, true repentance lay, not in the sacrificial offering of herds of cattle and the recital of interminable solemn prayers but in the observance of the Law. And the same may well be true for us, *mutatis mutandis*. Our knowledge has been vastly extended beyond what was comprehended by the Children of Israel; our way of living is utterly different from theirs. The laws of physical well-being that applied to them may, in some ways, be obsolete for us. Even so, our bodies are subject to immutable laws which we transgress at our peril. We know now how smallpox and bubonic plague can be suppressed, and we are acutely conscious of the punishment that is meted out to us if we disregard the conditions that hold those terrible evils in check. Merely to pray that we should not be afflicted might well mean suicide. Except the Christian Scientists, few of us would be willing to contend with an outbreak of smallpox by doing nothing beyond holding prayer meetings; if that were the only action we took, most of us would think we were indeed flying in the face of Providence, although in the midst of a smallpox epidemic prayer would most certainly bolster morale. Malaria can be stamped out by means of DDT, mepacrine, and improved hygiene; without these things the sincerest, most earnest missionary in tropical lands falls a victim: even Livingstone could not survive. And the same may well be true, I believe, of such contemporary scourges as cancer,

tuberculosis, infantile paralysis, Parkinson's disease, disseminated sclerosis, coronary thrombosis, intestinal ulcers, and other
maladies. We must learn the laws governing disease and obey
them.

This chimes, I suppose, with my earliest training. I was
brought up on the doctrine that Heaven helps those who help
themselves. God, I was taught, desires workers, not shirkers.
And I have a sneaking sympathy for Jeremy Cruncher, whose
complaint was that his wife was for ever "flopping" to pray
against him.

There is, I suggest, a real danger in making prayer seem too
easy, and a fatal temptation to use it to shelve our own
responsibilities. Few of us, for mysticism is a rare quality,
have any notion of all that prayer demands. In infancy we are
taught to repeat rigmaroles parrot fashion, and we go through
life imagining that this practice constitutes prayer. To imply
that the Churches today encourage the notion that prayer is
easy and irresponsible would be to misrepresent grotesquely
their teaching. It is the exact opposite that is the truth. They
insist that prayer is difficult and demanding, an exhausting
spiritual exercise, though one of which all human beings are
capable because of the mercy of God and His omnipresence.

I am left wondering, too, whether divine healing, psychic
healing, and faith healing are necessarily exclusive. Their
methods and claims seem to me to be almost identical, apart
from their basic assumptions. Nevertheless some people who
are willing to accept divine healing, with its ecclesiastical rites,
are intolerant of the other practices. And yet we know so
little of these extraordinary things that I, for one, hesitate to
accept one and not the others. "In my Father's house there are
many mansions," and it seems to me that the divine healers,
the faith healers, and the Spiritualist healers are all moving
to the same great end.

The experiments of Professor Rhine and his fellow-workers
in many countries have shown, from an angle entirely different
from that of both Spiritualism and orthodox religion, how
great are the potentialities of the human mind. Telepathy,

clairvoyance, prophetic dreams, the ability of the mind to move matter independently of any other agency—phenomena studied under laboratory conditions—are now well on the way to general acceptance by informed opinion. It is no surprise, therefore, to find the American physicist and Nobel prize-winner, Du Bose, writing: "There is less and less disposition to deny that there are psychic and spiritual forces as yet latent in human nature, of which we know nought whereunto the future development may reach."

Whately Carington, whose researches altered our whole conception of telepathy, argued in his book that our fundamental trouble today is an insufficient understanding of man's mind. And Rhine himself has exclaimed how shocking it is that we know the atom better than we know the mind that knows the atom. If, however, we could move on to wider knowledge and discover how to apply it, then, Rhine has said: "Science would have another extension to perception, one that would be more penetrative than all the instruments yet devised. No lurking disease, no impending epidemic, no obscure source of danger to society, could hide from the extra-sensorial insight directed to discover it. The location of the hidden wealth of the world, mineral and non-mineral, could be charted. What problems of the universe could be left long unsolved for lack of a means of observation?"

That is the promise held out by psychic research, parapsychology, Spiritualism, call it what you will, and I am confident it can be answered, though how and in what terms I cannot prophesy. The man of science and the man of religion, the philosopher and the medium, are at last linking together to explore the whole nature of man in body, mind, and spirit, just as they are beginning to join forces to aid him in sickness. This union can bring to fulfilment that extension to perception which Rhine describes. But that consummation of their endeavours can only be achieved by complete tolerance, good will, and understanding by all who are working in this field. Nothing that I have seen in the course of my inquiry makes me doubt that ultimately they will be successful.

BOOKS CONSULTED

E. E. Fournier D'Albe: *Life of Sir William Crookes.*

Dr. Rebecca Beard: *Everyman's Search.*

Prof. C. D. Broad: *Mind and Its Place in Nature.*

Henry Cadbury: *George Fox's Book of Miracles.*

Whately Carington: *Telepathy.*

J. Dickson Carr: *Life of Sir Arthur Conan Doyle.*

Charles Darwin: *The Origin of Species.*

Sir Arthur Conan Doyle: *History of Spiritualism.*

Lord Dowding: *The Dark Star.*

Lord Dowding: *Many Mansions.*

Harry Edwards: *Psychic Healing.*

C. L. Estrange Ewen: *Witch Hunting and Witch Trials.*

Canon L. W. Grensted: *Psychology and God.*

Hansard *passim.*

Harry Houdini: "A Magician Among the Spirits" in *The Case For and Against Psychical Belief* edited by Prof. C. Murchison.

Rev. W. R. Inge: *The Philosophy of Plotinus.*

Prof. J. Jastrow: "The Animus of Psychical Research" in *The Case For and Against Psychical Belief* edited by Prof. C. Murchison.

Rev. W. R. Matthews: *Psychical Research and Theology.*

W. Stainton Moses: *Spirit Teachings.*

Prof. William McDougall: *An Outline of Abnormal Psychology.*

H. Macgregor and M. V. Underhill: *The Psychic Faculties and Their Development.*

Father H. V. O'Neill: *Spiritualism* (with a preface by Archbishop Downey).

Prof. J. B. Rhine. *The Reach of the Mind.*

Prof. J. B. Rhine: *New Frontiers of the Mind.*

Elsie Salmon: *He Heals Today.*

Agnes Sanford: *The Healing Light.*

Society for Psychical Research: *Hints on Sitting with Mediums.*

T. Howard Somervell: *After Everest.*

Rev. C. Drayton Thomas: *Life Beyond Death.*

Rev. Herbert Thurston: *Spiritualism.*

G. N. M. Tyrrell: *The Personality of Man.*

Rev. Leslie D. Weatherhead: *Psychology, Religion and Healing.*

Dr. Carl Wickland: *Thirty Years Among the Dead.*

INDEX

INDEX